Tracy Letts in the Steppenwolf Theatre Company production of *Last of the Boys*.

LAST OF
THE BOYS

BY **STEVEN DIETZ**

★

DRAMATISTS
PLAY SERVICE
INC.

for Joe Sedlachek

LAST OF THE BOYS received its World Premiere at the McCarter Theatre Center (Emily Mann, Artistic Director; Jeffrey Woodward, Managing Director) in Princeton, New Jersey, opening September 7, 2004. It was directed by Emily Mann; the set design was by Eugene Lee; the costume design was by David Murin; the lighting design was by Jeff Croiter; the sound design was by Rob Milburn and Michael Bodeen; the producing director was Mara Isaacs; the dramaturg was Janice Paran; and the stage manager was Cheryl Mintz. The cast was as follows:

BEN	Joseph Siravo
JEETER	Tom Wopat
SALYER	Jenny Bacon
LORRAINE	Deborah Hedwall
THE YOUNG SOLDIER	Steven Boyer

LAST OF THE BOYS was subsequently produced by Steppenwolf Theatre Company (Martha Lavey, Artistic Director; David Hawkanson, Executive Director) in Chicago, Illinois, opening on September 15, 2005. It was directed by Rick Snyder; the set design was by Todd Rosenthal; the costume design was by Janice Pytel; the lighting design was by Ann G. Wrightson; the sound design was by Rob Milburn and Michael Bodeen; and the stage manager was Laura D. Glenn. The cast was as follows:

BEN	Tracy Letts
JEETER	John Judd
SALYER	Mariann Mayberry
LORRAINE	Amy Morton
THE YOUNG SOLDIER	Christopher McLinden

LAST OF THE BOYS was originally commissioned by San Jose Repertory Theatre (Timothy Near, Artistic Director; Alexandra Urbanowski, Managing Director) in San Jose, California.

CHARACTERS

BEN — a Vietnam vet, 50s
JEETER — Ben's friend, also a vet, 50s
SALYER — Jeeter's girlfriend, 35
LORRAINE — Salyer's mother, 50s
THE YOUNG SOLDIER — deceased, 19

PLACE

An abandoned trailer park.
Somewhere in the Great Central Valley of California.

TIME

The final summer of the twentieth century.

Neither anticipated that the cause of the conflict might cease with, or even before, the conflict itself should cease. Each looked for an easier triumph, and a result less fundamental and astounding.

—*Abraham Lincoln*
Second Inaugural, 1865

His regret cannot be huge enough to balance the books for our dead soldiers. The ghosts of those unlived lives circle close around Mr. McNamara. Surely he must, in every quiet and prosperous moment, hear the ceaseless whispers of those poor boys in the infantry, dying in the tall grass, platoon by platoon, for no purpose. What he took from them cannot be repaid by prime-time apology and stale tears, three decades late.

—The New York Times, *1995*

The other half of memory is sight.

—*Richard Hugo*

LAST OF THE BOYS

ACT ONE

Two Men and Time

*You might wonder who lives here. An old rusted trailer; a dirt
and gravel yard. Old trees forming a canopy behind. You got
lost out here, you'd need directions. You might be brave. Might
approach, calling out a little "hello." Or you might summon
a bit of common sense and give the whole place a wide berth.
You wouldn't be the first.*

*It's day. You see only the front of the trailer; the few weathered
steps that lead up to the single door. The yard itself is ringed with
piles of sandbags and an old rusted wire fence. And in the yard:
odd things scattered about. Not so much messy, as displaced. An
ironing board — open, its legs sitting atop a few weathered
metal crates. An ancient fridge. (Damn thing still works — the
warranty and salesman both long dead.) A big, round wash
basin sitting prominently atop a stack of cinder blocks. In the
center of the yard, a "fire pit" of some kind, which is surrounded
by a handful of rickety chairs that — like the land all around —
have seen better days. A good, warm Mexican blanket is tossed
over one of the chairs. A clothesline runs from one corner of the
trailer to a tall metal flagpole downstage. No flag is flying. Also,
near the trailer: a military green stand-up locker. Finally, at the
edge of the yard: a large rusty dumpster, its lid open and waiting.*

*In addition to the afternoon light, there's no doubt some music
in the air: maybe something like Mr. Dylan's "Subterranean
Homesick Blues" — cranked up loud.* *

* See Special Note on Songs and Recordings on copyright page.

You look and listen for a while … and then —

A man appears from the trailer, slamming the door behind him. Moves into the yard, holding a bottle of beer. Not a good beer. This is a point of contention. He moves around the yard a bit, wired, before maybe sitting in one of the rickety-ass chairs.

His name is Stephen Willoughby Stark. You'd know him as Jeeter. He's a vet. Vietnam. Our man Jeeter has lived hard in his fifty-plus years. Knocked about these amber waves for a good long time and left his name on an awful lot of lists. What you might not guess till you buy him his third shot is that he's a professor. Little college up in the redwoods. Teaches a course on "The Sixties." (It's come to that.) Writes a little poetry you wouldn't like. Plays in a shitty cover band. Dates coeds. It's a life. His summers are free, so Jeeter travels about, hither and yon, engaging in various "quests" that you'll more than likely hear all about. And he always ends up here: at the home of his best pal, his "top hombre," his "comrade in armchairs": Benjamin Lee Holloway. You'd know him as Ben. And chances are you'd like him. He's a builder. Used to work for a contractor, but couldn't abide a lesser man looking over his shoulder. Too much like Nam. Yeah, he's a vet, too. Around Jeeter's age. Nowadays, Ben works alone. Just a pile of wood and his tools and the whole day before him. Don't romanticize it; he doesn't.

This is Ben now — coming out of the trailer. He's got a beer, too — which he kills and tosses into the dumpster, with intent. He moves with purpose to the clothesline and removes the one item hanging there like a ghost: a clean, white dress shirt. From the military locker, he removes an iron. Plugs it into the long extension cord that emerges from under the trailer. Moves to the ironing board. Begins to iron the shirt.

Jeeter watches all of it, saying nothing.

Music fades out. It is strangely quiet. These men have known each other for thirty years and now you watch as they manage to say absolutely nothing to each other.

And then: as if there's been no break in their talk whatsoever —

JEETER. *(Hot.)* 'Cause you should have been there, okay?! You don't want to hear it — but *there it is —*
BEN. Jeet —
JEETER. *(Overlapping.)* — there it just no-doubt *is.*
BEN. *(Also hot.)* I told you why —
JEETER. Nothin' —
BEN. I told you why I wasn't there —
JEETER. That's nothin' — okay?! — what is this bullshit, Ben?
BEN. *(Overlapping from "okay.")* It's "nothin'" because you don't want to hear it — you don't want to listen to why I wasn't there —
JEETER. No, I *do* — I really *do* —
BEN. I don't *owe you this,* okay?! I don't *owe you a reason. (Beat. Breath.)*
JEETER. Wow. Okay. Let's take a minute to establish some basic ground rules; some facts about where things stand. This, if I'm not mistaken — if I'm not just a victim of your foul mood and your increasingly marginal beer — *this is still planet Earth.* Am I right?
BEN. *Forget it. (Ben irons, avidly. Jeeter keeps after him — a dog on a meat wagon.)*
JEETER. And as is the custom on Planet Earth, when a man's *father dies* — the son often is expected to make an appearance at the funeral. No matter how messy the past, how great the estrangement, there is this tacit understanding that a son can find the time to *drop a little dirt on the box. (Ben looks up at Jeeter, hard; then returns to his ironing.)* I drove *three days,* Ben. *Michigan,* man — who thought up *that place?* A state shaped like a sad man's head. Your sister and what's-his-face and the kids were there. Lotsa old photos and potato salad. Everybody really liked Sal.
BEN. Sal?
JEETER. Salyer. Her real name is Salyer.
BEN. Who the hell is that?
JEETER. I told you — I met her on the road. She came with me to Michigan.
BEN. You picked up a girl on the way to my dad's funeral?
JEETER. At least she *went.* And she talked to everyone. Wanted to know all about your dad, the war, why the hell you weren't there.
BEN. None of her damn business.

11

JEETER. That so?

BEN. You tell her that.

JEETER. *(Smiles.)* No, *you* tell her that. I'm bringin' her by tonight. You're gonna love this girl.

BEN. Jeet —

JEETER. I mean it, Ben — this girl — I'm tellin' you — I mean, you know me — you know me and women and don't say anything in response to that — but, really, Ben, this girl has …

BEN. Yeah?

JEETER. I'll get it.

BEN. Uh-huh.

JEETER. I'll *get it.* I'll get the word.

BEN. Uh-huh.

JEETER. This girl has … *gravitas. (Beat.)*

BEN. Uh-huh.

JEETER. That's Latin.

BEN. No kidding?

JEETER. "Importance — intensity — a vigorous *bearing.*"

BEN. Uh-huh.

JEETER. That's the word.

BEN. And you've known her …

JEETER. Seventeen days.

BEN. I see.

JEETER. That's nearly three weeks.

BEN. Yes, it is.

JEETER. Changed a tire on her car. She and her mom — stranded at the side of the road without a tire iron. I do my good deed — I turn to go — and she slips me her number.

BEN. Uh-huh.

JEETER. Weird thing.

BEN. Sounds that way.

JEETER. No, the weird thing — you with me?

BEN. Right here.

JEETER. The weird thing: It comes out that I'm a vet.

BEN. It "comes out"?

JEETER. Not a card you play with women, Ben. Not a *cologne* you want to wear —

BEN. And the point is — ?

JEETER. I mean, not that *you'd* know —

BEN. Jeet —

12

JEETER. — and we *won't get into that* — but any-hoo: It comes out that I'm a vet and now, *now* she gets interested. She's all over me like Nixon on a martini — a million questions about the-this and the-that of the war. *Bully for her,* I'm thinkin' — and *eureka for me:* a girl that's into grizzled old grunts. Thought I'd died and gone to Bangkok. *(Ben is finished with the shirt. It's perfect. He's good at this. He puts the shirt on a hanger and hangs it carefully in the military locker. Jeeter watches all of this.)* Okay.
BEN. Okay.
JEETER. Okay …
BEN. Okay?
JEETER. Okay — what's up with the shirt? *(Beat.)* I'm just asking. *(Beat.)* I'm just asking about the shirt.
BEN. *(Firm.)* There's nothing.
JEETER. Okay.
BEN. Nothing is up with the shirt.
JEETER. Okay.
BEN. Okay.
JEETER. It's nice. It's a nice shirt.
BEN. Thank you.
JEETER. "There is no man who cannot be improved by a clean, crisp white shirt."
BEN. *(Hot.)* Okay, see —
JEETER. What?
BEN. — You're doing it.
JEETER. Yeah, so —
BEN. You said you were done. Ever since you got here —
JEETER. *(Overlapping from "ever.")* Yeah, I know, but, hey —
BEN. It's troubling.
JEETER. Got it.
BEN. Troubling and embarrassing —
JEETER. Point taken.
BEN. This *quoting.* This *constant quoting* of *MY father.*
JEETER. It's A VOICE I HEAR.
BEN. Quote your *OWN father,* for chrissakes —
JEETER. And you would not believe — I hear it at the damnedest times. Like two nights ago, Sal and I are at this *techno-shamanism* workshop —
BEN. Enough, Jeet — okay?!
JEETER. Oh, god forbid your dad's words might *outlive him* by a

week or two —

BEN. This is NOT THE TIME, Jeet —

JEETER. *(Overlapping.)* God forbid a phrase gets turned in a way that *displeases you* — BAM: You're the "WORD CZAR" — BAM: You're the "LINGO POLICE" on matters of this kind —

BEN. *(Overlapping from "LINGO.")* "YOUR DAD ALWAYS SAID" — "YOUR DAD ALWAYS SAID" — *YOU MET THE MAN ONCE!* — YOU SPENT *THREE DAYS* WITH HIM — THEN YOU GO TO HIS FUNERAL AND TALK LIKE YOU WERE HIS BEST PAL IN THE WORLD —

JEETER. *HE WAS RIGHT ABOUT THE SHIRT! (Silence. They settle, regroup, reload.)* Didn't mean to go there, buddy.

BEN. Uh-huh.

JEETER. Didn't mean to *"harsh your mellow." (Pause. Ben is putting the iron away. Re: the shirt.)* Starch?

BEN. Light.

JEETER. Right.

BEN. Very light.

JEETER. Like Daddy always said. *(Ben shoots him a look — but now it's a rope, not a dagger. They sip beers. There it is: the ease.)* Saw a lot of photos. *(Off Ben's look.)* Back in Michigan.

BEN. Yeah, you said.

JEETER. On that shelf by your dad's workbench. *(Beat.)* Nice shelf. Lot a photos there. *(Beat, angling for a smile out of Ben.)* God, you were a cute little kid — the hell happened to you?

BEN. He had a photo of me there?

JEETER. Bunch of 'em. Little league. Ice-fishing. Graduation.

BEN. And later?

JEETER. Huh?

BEN. Anything after that?

JEETER. What am I — your *spy?* Go there yourself and *have a look-see.*

BEN. *Forget it.*

JEETER. No.

BEN. I said —

JEETER. *Nothing. (Beat.)* There was nothing after that. No photos after that.

BEN. *(Pause.)* Okay.

JEETER. Thought there'd be one of you in uniform. Every parent has their kid's service photo gathering dust somewhere, don't they?

— but not your old man.

BEN. Okay.

JEETER. I looked, Ben. Asked around. It's gone. *(Silence. Jeeter is looking in the direction of the flagpole.)* You've got no flag?

BEN. Huh?

JEETER. You got a flagpole and no flag?

BEN. Uh-huh.

JEETER. You got nothing to *fly,* is that it?

BEN. Looks that way.

JEETER. *(Happily.)* Not to worry — I brought you one.

BEN. I do not need one of your "Rainbow Unicorn Zodiac Peace" flags, okay?

JEETER. That's not what I brought you.

BEN. Yeah, right. *(Jeeter goes to a corner of the yard where his backpack sits, and retrieves something that's been sitting, unseen, behind it: a suitcase — circa 1962, mint condition. Jeeter sets the suitcase in front of Ben.)*

JEETER. Your dad was a vet. When they buried him, there was a flag. Your sister said you'd want it. *(Ben says nothing.)* You don't want it?

BEN. Jeet —

JEETER. You don't want the flag from your *old man's coffin?* —

BEN. JEETER —

JEETER. — *Jesus, what's up with you?* I bring you his suitcase — not a scratch on it, the man must have *polished it after every trip* —

BEN. Listen — I don't care what you —

JEETER. *(Overlapping.)* — I take it and I fill it with shit I thought you'd want because *excuse me* but *you weren't there* when your sister and what's-his-face started picking over the house — so I just tried to *save you a few things. (Beat, sharp.) Fine* — don't open it — throw it away, if you want — I don't care. *(And Jeeter storms off into, or behind, the trailer. Silence. Ben stares at the suitcase. Then, he stands, lifts the suitcase, carries it to the dumpster and — without a moment's hesitation — tosses it in. Ben starts back to his chair and begins to sit down. Stops. And then heads right back to the dumpster and retrieves the damn thing. Sets it once again in the yard. Stares at it. Kneels. Opens it. Looks inside. From the suitcase, Ben removes a small framed picture. As he does so, Jeeter pokes his head back into the yard …)* Knew you'd want that. Look at them, huh? You ever seen two people so damn young and sharp and ready for the world?

Beautiful, really.

BEN. This was at Ford Motor.

JEETER. Nineteen-sixty. *(Ben continues to look at the picture.)* Your dad and his boss: Robert S. McNamara. Look like brothers, don't they? Right down to the suit and tie. *(Re: the suitcase.)* Which, by the way, are in there, too. *(Pause, smiles.)* Always thought you were crazy to enlist, old buddy ... then I saw that picture. It's the "domino theory," right? Your dad worships McNamara — you worship your dad — and so *off you go.*

BEN. *(Turns to Jeeter.)* Why would you bring this? *(Jeeter sips his beer. Then ...)*

JEETER. I'm at this *vortex* a couple summers back. I know that's a word that scares you — like "chakra" and "tofu" and "commitment." But, listen: I'm at this vortex with a *guide.* Go to any bar in the American southwest and hit on a brunette in cowboy boots and thirty bucks sez you've found yourself a *"guide."* Her name was Angel. Black hair like a shroud she could bury you in. Claimed to be a Hopi (found out later she was Greek and from Indianapolis but that's not the story) — the thing is: She told me if I sat there and cleared my mind, I would *channel someone.* The vortex would bring me a voice — a voice I'd been seeking or lacking — this voice would not only speak to me — no, it would *inhabit me* and *transform me* and *guide me* — because *this is the thing,* Jeeter, she kept saying to me on top of that mountain: *We become the people we need. (Silence. Jeeter's eyes are now closed.)*

BEN. And...?

JEETER. Ssshh ... *(More silence. Jeeter's eyes remain closed. He's away somewhere. Ben puts the picture back inside the suitcase. Closes it. Stares at Jeeter — who has not moved. Ben goes to the fridge, grabs a couple of fresh beers. Carries them to Jeeter. Ben gently removes the empty from Jeeter's hand — Jeeter does not stir an inch — and replaces it with a fresh one. Then, Ben throws Jeeter's empty into the dumpster — and the crash causes Jeeter to slowly open his eyes. Ben stands/sits near his friend, his own beer in hand. He waits. Two men and time. Jeeter stares front. Stares at the full beer in his hand. Turns and stares at Ben. Quietly:)* Hey.

BEN. Hey. *(Silence.)*

JEETER. Am I okay?

BEN. You're fine. *(Silence.)*

JEETER. I was saying something ...

BEN. It don't matter.

JEETER. No.

BEN. It don't mean nothin'. *(They drink. They ease. Jeeter's tone brightens.)*

JEETER. You're all that's left.

BEN. Huh?

JEETER. The last trailer standing.

BEN. Yeah.

JEETER. What about that lady with the double-wide? Had all those cats named after Vonnegut books?

BEN. Held out till last year.

JEETER. Then she took the money —

BEN. Yeah.

JEETER. Packed up her trailer —

BEN. Uh-huh.

JEETER. And got the *hell* out. *(Ben nods. Sits.)* So, what's stopping you?

BEN. I like it here.

JEETER. On a *Superfund site?!*

BEN. That was never proven.

JEETER. It was never *proven?!* It was never proven because the company swooped in —

BEN. That was —

JEETER. *(Overlapping.)* Swooped in and *bought the whole town* before the EPA could lower the boom.

BEN. *Conjecture.*

JEETER. Huh?

BEN. That's conjecture.

JEETER. Ben: Are you familiar with the word *"isotope."* There's shit in this ground that'll be glowin' when the sun flares out.

BEN. Let it go, Jeet —

JEETER. BEN —

BEN. Jeet —

JEETER. — TOM BROKAW CAME HERE.

BEN. Oh, happy day.   JEETER. THAT IS NOT
                                                        CONJECTURE.

JEETER. When Tom Brokaw comes to your town and scrinches up his forehead and they play that "Really Concerned American" music — you KNOW there's something going on.

BEN. People got what they wanted.

JEETER. Unbelievable —

BEN. *(Overlapping.)* The ones who wanted the money, took it. I wanted to be alone — and I am.

JEETER. You're living with toxins.

BEN. I used to live with *you*. *(There it is. Beers are sipped; the mood shifts.)*

JEETER. You're gonna love Sal.

BEN. Okay.

JEETER. And no comments about her clothes.

BEN. Okay.

JEETER. I *mean it.*

BEN. *Okay. (Beat.)* What *about* her clothes?

JEETER. It's not the kind, it's the *amount.* A lot of clothes. She just wears a lot of clothes — okay?!

BEN. Okay.

JEETER. She's being followed.

BEN. Uh-huh.

JEETER. Or thinks she is. Her ex-boyfriend. Long story. Nasty break-up — *god, the things that transpire,* huh? — so, now she's on the run, sort of.

BEN. *(Lightly.) Sort of?*

JEETER. This guy is obsessed. Might be following her.

BEN. Uh-huh.

JEETER. She's *scared,* Ben.

BEN. And is this tied into the clothes?

JEETER. No, this is NOT — JESUS —

BEN. *(Overlapping.)* I'm just tryin' to put two and two —

JEETER. *(Overlapping.)* All you need to know is that her name is Sal and that I don't want you to say it.

BEN. Say what?

JEETER. *The very next thing you want to say.* Here's what we do: Sal and I stop by tonight after the concert — you smile and nod and make nice — a little whiskey, a little chit-chat, very civil, very no big deal — and then —

BEN. *(With a laugh.)* You've got this all *scripted?*

JEETER. *(Overlapping.)* — And then in the morning I come by and you sit me down with an old donut and a cup of bad coffee and you say: "Jeet — *marry that girl.* Put a ring on her finger and clean your apartment and settle your sorry old ass *down." That's* what I want you to say. *(Beat. Ben smiles. Jeeter grows suspicious.) What?*

BEN. Nothing.

JEETER. This amuses you?!

BEN. You're a fucking wreck!

JEETER. I am not —

BEN. You are *wasted* over this girl!

JEETER. *(Smiles.)* Okay, then: tonight. After the concert.

BEN. I'll be here.

JEETER. You got any paint?

BEN. Why?

JEETER. I need a new sign.

BEN. Oh, jesus —

JEETER. I can't go the concert without my sign.

BEN. What happened to your old one?

JEETER. Tokyo. Security took it.

BEN. You followed that band to Tokyo?

JEETER. Singapore, Manila, Budapest —

BEN. It never works, Jeeter.

JEETER. Okay, no, not yet, but —

BEN. *(Overlapping.)* Jeet: The sign *never ever works.*

JEETER. You're right.

BEN. *Thank you.*

JEETER. But I still gotta do it. *(Ben and Jeeter clink bottles — kill their beers — and fling their empties at the dumpster, where they crash, side by side. Nice.)* Okay.

BEN. There it is.

JEETER. There it just no-doubt *is. (Lights shift and music plays: some kind of great, driving anthem like the EARLY Fleetwood Mac's "Oh Well."* You can crank it.*

Ben moves to his chair and settles in — alone with his thousand-yard stare, as —

Lights shift from afternoon to night. The yard is now drenched in moonlight. The only other light comes from inside Ben's trailer.

As music continues, Ben stands and heads inside, to bed. After a moment, the light inside the trailer goes off.

Darkness. Moonlight. Music out, leaving only the sound of crickets. And then —

The low drone of distant helicopters is heard, and —

From the shadows emerges: a Young Soldier. And I mean young.

---

* See Special Note on Songs and Recordings on copyright page.

19

Twenty at most; looks all of twelve. In his dress uniform — so clean and pressed; a penny that just left the mint.

The Young Soldier moves into the moonlit yard, with purpose. He goes directly to the suitcase. Carries it to [or near] the ironing board. Opens it.

As he does so: An odd, white light begins to illuminate the surface of the ironing board from directly above. The rest of the yard remains dark.

With efficiency and precision, the Young Solder now removes the following items from the suitcase — and places them atop the ironing board in a neat row: the framed picture we saw earlier ... a thin black necktie ... a black suit coat ... a leather eyeglasses case.

Next: The Young Soldier moves to the wash basin. He lifts a large, full bucket which is next to the basin — and slowly pours the water into the basin.

As he does so: An odd, white light [similar to that on the ironing board] begins to illuminate the wash basin from directly above.

The drone of helicopters continues to pound, growing closer/more intense, as —

The Young Soldier, finished with this task, takes a moment to lower his head and stare down into the shimmering water ... and, at the moment when he lifts his head back up, the following things happen almost simultaneously:

A jet is heard, very loud, strafing the sky — The light in the trailer goes on — Ben screams out —)

BEN. *(From inside trailer.)* JEETER?! *(Ben throws open the trailer door —)* JEETER, IS THAT YOU — ?! *(— and sees the Young Soldier.*

They stare at one another. Ben is frozen, frightened, caught.

Now: The Young Soldier moves with purpose to the military locker. Opens it. Removes the white shirt.

Ben remains motionless; watching.

The Young Soldier stands behind the ironing board, holding the shirt out in front of him ... ready to help Ben put it on.

Ben takes a step toward the Young Soldier, curious — then stops.

The Young Soldier nods.

Music begins again, under ... perhaps the slow, reflective middle section of "Oh Well" ... quietly now, joining the distant drone of the helicopters.

Slowly, Ben approaches the ironing board ... looks at the items arranged there ... and now, cautiously, Ben allows the Young Soldier to help him put on the white shirt.

As Ben buttons the shirt — the Young Soldier readies the tie.

As Ben ties the tie — the Young Soldier readies the jacket.

After helping Ben put on the jacket — the Young Soldier hands Ben the leather glasses case.

Ben stares at him; the Young Soldier, again, nods.

Ben removes wire eyeglasses from the case ... and puts them on, as —

The Young Soldier places a single sheet of white paper on the ironing board. Then, he steps aside.

Ben slowly takes his place behind the ironing board — as though standing at a podium.

Ben lifts the framed photograph and gives it a long look. Ben looks back at the Young Soldier — who, once again, nods.

Now: Ben lowers his head and looks down at the paper. Takes a deep breath. And when he lifts his head —

A jet strafes the sky —

A hot white light hits Ben's face —

Music stops, instantly —

And, peering out into the audience, Ben speaks. NOTE: This is not intended to be an "impersonation" of Robert S. McNamara. It should, instead, be thought of as a "channeling": McNamara's words pouring out of the man we know as Ben.) Good evening. *(Consulting the paper before him.)* Earlier tonight the President told the nation the United States would take appropriate action to respond to the unprovoked attacks on U.S. Naval vessels in the Gulf of Tonkin. Furthermore, the United States has taken the precaution of moving substantial military reinforcements to Southeast Asia. *(Points to an unseen questioner.)* Question. *(Beat — he listens.)* No, I cannot name the bases that were attacked. *(Points to another questioner.)* No, I can't tell you how many bases. *(Impatient — points to another.)* Yes, the attack is currently underway — *(Interrupting another question.)* — and no, I can't give you any more information. *(Turns to another questioner.)* There have been no casualties so far. *(And another. With growing force.)* No — this does not mean that ground forces are being put into South Vietnam. It means that we are reinforcing our forces with such additional force as we believe to be required — and have placed on alert such forces as we believe to be necessary. *(Looks around the room, as he puts the piece of paper back in his coat.)* One more question. *(But the question does not come. The white light is vanishing. The moonlit yard and the sound of crickets is returning, but —*

Ben continues to stand there, ready to continue —) I said: one more question. Are you there?! *ONE MORE QUESTION.*

SALYER. Okay, here's one: Is this where the Unabomber used to live? *(And he sees her. At the edge of the yard. Maybe she's been watching from the shadows. She's got a hundred questions. But they don't come out. Not yet. Only this —)* Hi. *(He stares at her. Frozen. This is Sal, of course. Salyer. [It will be explained.] You'd be struck by the fierce beauty of her face. And you might even win a smile from it — though they don't come easy. The rest of her is covered over — every square inch — in layers of dark clothing. Long sleeves, high collars, sheer gloves. A long black coat or sweater. Always. [It will be explained.])* You're Ben. *(He takes off the glasses.)*

BEN. Yeah.

SALYER. Sal.

BEN. *Salyer.*

SALYER. Very good.

BEN. I was briefed.

SALYER. So … *(Out it comes.)* … what the hell are you doing? *(He simply stares at her. No explanation is forthcoming. Instead: Ben is now taking off the coat, the tie, the white shirt — putting all the evidence away inside the military locker.)*

BEN. Where's Jeeter?

SALYER. Looking for something in the van. Who are you talking to? *(No response.)* Okay — hey — maybe you're just some kind of —

BEN. *(Sharp.)* I'm not talking to *anyone*, okay?!

SALYER. Your sister says "hi." *(This stops him.)* Nice lady. We got good and drunk together after they put your dad in the ground. I bitched about my mother and your sister bitched about you and then we went outside and watched the northern lights and she said she needed a hug and I gave her one and then I guess we were sort of making out for a while under those freaky, swirly lights and then she had to go throw up and I said call me and then it was morning. *(Beat.)* I love funerals. *(He says nothing. She sits.)* You're a handyman.

BEN. *What?*

SALYER. Jeeter said that's what you do. You're a handyman.

BEN. I'm a *carpenter.*

SALYER. I see.

BEN. There's a difference.

SALYER. Which is?

BEN. I don't *fix* things. I *build* things.

SALYER. I see.

BEN. Okay.

SALYER. A carpenter.

BEN. Right.

SALYER. Like Jesus.

BEN. Again: There's a difference. *(Ben moves away. Gets a beer.)* How was the concert?

SALYER. How many times has Jeeter seen that band? He said two hundred. *Two hundred times?*

BEN. Sounds about right.

SALYER. Who can do that? Who can go see the Stones two hundred times?!

BEN. That's Jeeter.

SALYER. And the *sign* — what is the deal with the *sign?*

BEN. Did he make it up front?

SALYER. For about thirty seconds — then security bounced us back to the cheap seats — Jeeter screaming at them — fighting with them over the sign —

BEN. That sign is one of his great quests.

SALYER. Yeah, well —

BEN. You should know that.

SALYER. Oh, should I?

BEN. I mean, if you're gonna — *(Stops.)*

SALYER. Gonna ... what?

BEN. You should just know that. *(Okay, this got weird, she's thinking. Where's this going? And where the hell is Jeeter?)* How'd they look?

SALYER. Who?

BEN. Mick and the boys.

SALYER. How did they *look?*

BEN. Yeah.

SALYER. Like cold pizza you forgot to throw out. *(Jeeter enters, dragging a large sign. He drops it face down on the ground before we have a chance to read it. He takes off a weathered backpack and begins avidly rummaging through it as he speaks.)*

JEETER. Damnit! — I can't find the damn thing — not anywhere. Tore the van apart. It's *gone.*

BEN. *(What?)* Yeah, okay. Want a beer?

JEETER. Little souvenir of the road — found the damn thing outside Sedona — just ask Sal — *(Barely looking up at them.)* — Oh, Ben, this is Sal — Sal, this is —

BEN. We did this.   SALYER. Got it.

JEETER. — And when I saw this thing — *no hesitation* — I said to the guy, this lapsed Mormon with a ferret on his shoulder — sign out front: "Souvenirs. Espresso. Astral Projection." — I said "Give me that for my friend, Ben." *No hesitation* —

BEN. Hey, don't worry about —

JEETER. *(Overlapping.)* — BUT NOW WHERE THE HELL IS IT? *(And Jeeter's hands are back inside that backpack, dumping out its contents, still searching.)*

BEN. *(To Salyer.)* He gets stuck.

SALYER. Huh?

BEN. On something — any little thing — he gets stuck.

SALYER. Don't I know it.

BEN. Hit the needle all you want — it won't jump the groove.

JEETER. What is that?

SALYER. Nothing.

JEETER. What are you going on about?

SALYER. We're not   JEETER. All the time,
"going on about"   going on, going on
anything —   about me —

BEN. Forget it, Jeet —

JEETER. No, I want to know —

SALYER. Stuck.

JEETER. What?

SALYER. You get *stuck on things* —

JEETER. PEOPLE —

SALYER. And you can't let go —

JEETER. People are NOT FAUCETS.

BEN. Jeet, c'mon, it doesn't matter —

JEETER. *(Overlapping.)* NO — GODDAMNIT — I WON'T BE TURNED ON AND OFF LIKE A — LIKE A FRIGGIN' — LIKE SOME KIND OF FRIGGIN' FUCKIN' FAUCET! — BECAUSE I LOVE HER, BEN! — I LOVE THIS WOMAN! — BUT I'LL BE DAMNED IF I'M GONNA LET ANYBODY JUST — *(Abrupt stop. Let it all stop here. Salyer looks away. Jeeter stares at Ben, then he winds up and throws the backpack to the ground — BOOM. And, there we are. Silence.)*

BEN. So … the concert was good? *(Jeeter just shakes his head.)* Anybody see the sign?

JEETER. *(Tone brightens.)* Maybe Keith. I think maybe Keith did.

Mick was blinded by all these skinny girls with cameras — a million little wiggling things with big flashing heads. Like a jar of sperm on vacation. And *young?* — god these girls were young enough to be his ... *girlfriend. Boo koo babysans.*

BEN. How long are you gonna do this?

JEETER. These are my guys, Ben — you know that —

BEN. Yeah, but Jeet —

JEETER. *(Overlapping).* And I gotta be straight with 'em — I gotta drag this sign to every concert I can until I know for sure they've *seen it.*

BEN. And you think that'll do the trick?

JEETER. It's got to. *(Jeeter lifts/turns the sign so that we see it for the first time. In big, block letters it reads: JUST STOP.)* They're the greatest fucking band of all time — but, hey: *Enough is enough.* TI-I-I-IME is NOT on their side — *no, it ain't.*

BEN. Well. Good luck.

JEETER. *(To Ben, with enthusiasm.)* Been showin' Salyer around the Valley. Redding to Bakersfield — the biggest damn farm in the world. *(To Salyer:)* Great place, huh? A little barren, a little toxic — but, hey, Ben guards his hootch like the good soldier he was. Not an easy job, though: *A waste is a terrible thing to mind. (Groan. Jeeter laughs. Sal smiles. Laughing:)* Oh, that's bad, huh?! Isn't that bad?!

SALYER. Yes, it is. *(And now Sal is kissing Jeeter.)* Really bad.

JEETER. *(Still laughing.)* God, I'm worse than Sammy — *(To Ben.)* Remember what a joker that Sammy was?

SALYER. Bathroom?

BEN. Inside. *(Salyer starts in.)*

JEETER. *God, that Sammy* — this one time —

BEN. *(To Salyer.)* If you're cold ... *(She stops, turns back.)* There's a blanket there. If you're cold.

SALYER. I'm not cold. *(She stares at him. Goes inside. Jeeter's mood instantly changes.)*

JEETER. *What did I say to you?!*

BEN. She looked cold.

JEETER. *She's not cold.* She dresses that way.

BEN. Okay.

JEETER. I told you that.

BEN. Okay.

JEETER. Damnit —

BEN. *Okay.*

JEETER. This is not us.

BEN. Huh?

JEETER. Don't judge us on this. We're not having a good night.

BEN. Uh-huh.

JEETER. We can be better. We're usually better. *(Beat.)* It's *you.*

BEN. Huh.

JEETER. She's all weird about meeting you. Everything I told her.

BEN. What's that mean?

JEETER. Nothing.

BEN. What's the *everything* you've told her?

JEETER. She *went to the funeral, Ben.* She was bound to *learn some things.*

BEN. So, what did she learn?

JEETER. Nothing that's not true. *(A hard silence.)* He was a great man, your Dad. *(Ben moves away —)* Never forget the last time I saw him. We'd finished our interview. He's in the laundry room. Busy. Always busy. And I watched that man *fold a fitted sheet. Perfectly.* Not a crease; corners sharp as a knife. *(Beat.) Shit.* I don't know *ANYONE* who can fold a fitted sheet.

BEN. What are you gonna do with that?

JEETER. Huh?

BEN. That interview.

JEETER. *(Returns to his backpack.)* Oh, hell, I don't know. Maybe crank out a little "scholarly article" for some cheap-ass magazine — *The Granola Quarterly*, or some such thing — somethin' to get the dean off my ass — *(From a pocket of his backpack, Jeeter produces something. Eureka.)* Hey: You're in luck! This is the thing I told you about — from Sedona. It's a little snowy paperweight thing — and you're thinking they're a dime a dozen, right?, but you would be WRONG, because LOOK AT THIS: See the little soldier in the rice paddy? — and the little Huey taking off? — the little mountain that says "Vietnam" in Hollywood-sign font? And look — *(He turns it over and back. It "snows.")* Orange! It snows Orange! *Tell me* you've seen anything like that! *(Hands it to Ben. Ben looks at the fucking thing. Jeeter is beaming.)* Guy only had one of them. I grabbed it before this leather-faced Earth mother could get her grubby turquoise paws on it — *(Stops, beat.)* You don't like it. *(No response.)* Go ahead. Break my heart.

BEN. Was this near that vortex?

JEETER. Huh?

BEN. That place you went to "hear a voice" —
JEETER. With Angel —
BEN. Yeah, right —
JEETER. To have that voice *inhabit me — transform me —*
BEN. Yeah —
JEETER. Right —
BEN. *Did it? (Beat.)* Did it do that? Did that happen? *(Beat.)*
JEETER. Since when do you care about all that *woo-woo* shit? *(Pause.)*
BEN. I *don't*, okay? *(Ben sets the snow globe down somewhere. Moves away.)*
JEETER. Okay … *(Long silence. Ben is staring off.)* Did I not say "yes" to that beer?
BEN. No, you did not.
JEETER. I wish to say "yes" at this time.
BEN. Request granted.
JEETER. *("33" — a Vietnamese beer.)* Ba moui ba.
BEN. *Ba moui ba.*
JEETER. "When're we out, Sergeant?"
BEN. "They say we'll be out by Christmas."
JEETER. Thanks be to god. *(Ben starts for the fridge.)*
BEN. Did she *fall in*, or what?
JEETER. Who?
BEN. The love of your life.
JEETER. She's got a lot to deal with, Ben.
BEN. Yeah, okay.
JEETER. Keep that in mind.
BEN. She made out with my sister.
JEETER. *Man.*
BEN. After the funeral.
JEETER. *Man, I always wanted to do that.* I always wanted to make out with your sister.
BEN. Yeah, well.
JEETER. And, unlike Salyer, *I really would have kissed her.*
BEN. You're saying she didn't?
JEETER. Salyer tends to "see things." I mean, god knows I love her to death — but she's been known to kinda make up stuff that sorta really *isn't there.*
BEN. Like this guy that's after her.
JEETER. No — *that's* real. I know for a fact that's for real.

27

BEN. Yeah, okay —

JEETER. Even tonight — she thought she saw him at the concert.

BEN. *(Sarcastic.)* I'll keep an eye out. *(And Ben has gone into the trailer. Jeeter sits, sips his beer. While maybe singing/humming a bit of a favorite Stones song — he lifts the little snowy paperweight and enjoys the orange snowfall, as, unseen to him — a woman appears in the yard. Her name is Lorraine. 'Bout the same age as Ben and Jeeter. Tough as a four-day-old steak. No-nonsense clothes. And, hidden behind her back: a very large tire iron. Jeeter jumps when she speaks. So would you.)*

LORRAINE. It's *"Jeeter,"* right?

JEETER. Whoa.

LORRAINE. Your name.

JEETER. Huh?

LORRAINE. Remember me?

JEETER. Should I?

LORRAINE. *This funny to you?*

JEETER. Not at all.

LORRAINE. Hell kind of name is "Jeeter"?

JEETER. A nickname.

LORRAINE. Is that so?

JEETER. A *nickname* kind of name.

LORRAINE. You remember me now?

JEETER. Uh —

LORRAINE. You did me a favor. My car had a flat. I didn't have a tire iron. You pulled over. Helped me out. Got me and my daughter on our way.

JEETER. Oh, right …

LORRAINE. Thanks.

JEETER. No problem.

LORRAINE. I've been looking for you. I wanted to return this. *(She lifts the tire iron. He sees it.)* Hold out your *head.*

JEETER. Whoa — okay — *(Lorraine moves into the yard like she owns the place.)*

LORRAINE. I don't know who I'm gonna clock *first* — her or you. *(And with this, she takes a swing at his head — as Jeeter gets the hell out of the way.)*

JEETER. What are you talking about?!

LORRAINE. You took my daughter and I'm gonna take her back.

JEETER. *(Forcing a laugh.)* I did not "take" your daughter. We went for a drive.

LORRAINE. That was three weeks ago.

JEETER. Seventeen days.

LORRAINE. Is she inside?

JEETER. She GAVE ME HER NUMBER.

LORRAINE. Wish I could say that sets you apart from every other two-legged thing with a pecker — but no such luck. This your "home"?

JEETER. No.

LORRAINE. Just "squatting"?

JEETER. What the hell are —

LORRAINE. *(Overlapping.)* Or maybe you've got the owners tied up inside. Little insignias on their foreheads — mumbling to themselves — stirring up the Kool-Aid.

JEETER. I'm a PROFESSOR, okay?!

LORRAINE. And I'm Miss America.

JEETER. *(Approaching her with caution.)* I'm an associate professor of humanities at the College of the Redwoods — I teach a nationally recognized course entitled: "The Sixties: A Paradigm of *Non-Violent Revolt*" — *(He grabs the tire iron away from Lorraine.)* — and this trailer is the home of my friend, Ben Holloway — and, yes, your daughter is here — *(The door to the trailer swings open. It's Ben.)*

BEN. Hey, Jeet —

JEETER. *(Quick.)* Tell Sal I need to see her.

BEN. I can't.

JEETER. Huh?

BEN. She's gone. *(Beat.)*

JEETER. She's *what? (And now Lorraine is marching off into the shadows behind the trailer, saying —)*

LORRAINE. *(Flat.)* Perfect. *(And now Jeeter is rushing off toward his van, saying —)*

JEETER. Sal? SALYER?! *(And now a jet strafes the sky again, and — intermittent sounds of distant mortar fire are heard, as — the Young Soldier enters from the shadows — again, with purpose. He carries an official-looking binder.)*

THE YOUNG SOLDIER. Good evening, Mr. Secretary. I have the briefing books you asked for.

BEN. *(Immediate, with an edge.)* What is this? *What do you want with me? (But, the Young Soldier does not stop moving. He sets the binder on the ironing board. Opens it. The Young Soldier produces five black-and-white photographs from the binder. During the following, he clips them to the clothesline — displaying them.)*

THE YOUNG SOLDIER. As you predicted, word of the bombings travelled quickly. *(Off Ben's look.)* The petroleum facilities. At Hanoi and Haiphong. I have the photographs you requested, as well. There are five of them. We received them this morning. *(The Young Soldier now produces the leather glasses case and offers it to Ben.)* Here you are, Mr. Secretary. *(Ben takes the glasses from the Young Soldier's hands. The Young Soldier moves to the photos on the clothesline. Using a portable work-light or clip-light in the yard: He illuminates them.)* I must tell you, sir: There have been many calls of concern. As the photos indicate, the areas that were destroyed were *civilian centers.* Both of them. There will no doubt be questions about that. *(At this, Ben puts on the glasses. During the following: Ben approaches the photos. Looks at them, closely.)* Mr. Secretary: Was there any attempt to *warn* the civilian population?

BEN. To *warn* them?

THE YOUNG SOLDIER. Yes, sir.

BEN. There was no *special effort* to warn them, no.

THE YOUNG SOLDIER. I see.

BEN. This attack happened in *daylight,* did it not?

THE YOUNG SOLDIER. Yes, sir.

BEN. Then the civilians had *every opportunity to be aware of it.*

THE YOUNG SOLDIER. But, sir — *(Ben now begins to pull the photos down from the clothesline — one after another.)*

BEN. *(Growing more certain, more definitive.)* I want to emphasize what I have said before: Our objectives are not to destroy the Communist government of North Vietnam; they are not to destroy the people of North Vietnam; they are not to provide a basis on which South Vietnam may become a military ally of the West. They are limited *solely* to permitting the South Vietnamese people to *shape their own destiny. (Ben hands the photos back to the Young Soldier.)*

THE YOUNG SOLDIER. And as to the question on the Senate floor —

BEN. What question is that?

THE YOUNG SOLDIER. If we are massing troops and carrying out bombing raids, why have we not declared war on North Vietnam?

BEN. *(Strong.)* There is nothing in modern international law which requires a state to declare war before engaging in hostilities against another state.

THE YOUNG SOLDIER. But, Mr. Secretary, isn't it true that —

BEN. *(Overlapping.)* I want to make it perfectly clear that the attacks of this morning are part of our policy of *exercising military RESTRAINT in North Vietnam. Is that clear? (But the Young Soldier does not respond. Military sounds begin to give way to crickets, once again …)* I said: Is that CLEAR?! *(The Young Soldier is, in fact, looking past Ben — to a figure in the shadows, behind Ben.)*

THE YOUNG SOLDIER. May I help you? *(And Salyer slowly steps out of the shadows. She keeps her distance. Ben turns, stares at her, does not move.)* Did you have a question for the Secretary? *(Silence.)*

SALYER. Umm …

THE YOUNG SOLDIER. If so, I'd be glad to convey it to him. *(Salyer simply stares at him, at Ben. Again: There are a million questions, but they don't come.)* Is there a question?

SALYER. Uh … no. Thank you. *(The Young Soldier nods. Turns. And leaves, taking the binder and photographs with him. Silence. Ben's gotta be wondering what the hell Salyer's going to say about this. But she simply says:)* Hi.

BEN. Jeeter's out looking for you. *(Ben moves now — puts the glasses away — maybe gets a beer. Salyer never takes her eyes off him.)*

SALYER. You want to ask, don't you?

BEN. *What?*

SALYER. About my clothes.

BEN. No.

SALYER. Go ahead — you can ask.

BEN. I really could care less why you —

SALYER. *Tattoos.* All over. I mean: *all over.*

BEN. Okay.

SALYER. My ex-boyfriend did them. Worked on me for weeks.

BEN. So why are you hiding them? *(Pause. Eye to eye.)*

SALYER. Do you believe in ghosts, Ben? *(He stares at her. Then starts for the trailer — Stopping him:)* Yeah. I don't believe in 'em either. Except when I *see 'em.* And, oh man, I see 'em. I saw 'em in Michigan. I saw 'em at the concert. And I saw 'em *here.* Jeeter thinks I'm making it all up. Funny, huh? — of all people — Jeeter — Captain Vortex — and, hey, you know, that's what I love about him: that he absolutely *expects the unbelievable to happen.* He'd just rather it not happen to *me. (And Lorraine is back in the yard.)*

31

LORRAINE. *(Seeing Salyer.)* Well howdy-do: *It's alive. (Upon seeing her, Salyer stops in her tracks.)* Okay — I can get us "stand-by" out of Modesto tomorrow morning. Or what they *call* "stand-by" nowadays — which is basically "build your own plane with what you've got in your purse." C'mon, baby. We'll get a hotel by the airport and make an early start. *(Salyer does not budge.)* Oh, now we're *not talking.* What memories *that* brings back. *(To Ben.)* I'm the Mom.

SALYER. So — what? — you've been *following me?*

LORRAINE. Not at all. I let the credit card people do that. A nice Mrs. Watkins calls me every day and tells me where you and your boyfriend are spending my money. Madison, Austin, Boulder, Sedona —

SALYER. Look —

LORRAINE. Did you buy Mommy some nice *wind chimes?*

SALYER. Whatever your plan is —

LORRAINE. My *plan?*

SALYER. Whatever it is: I'm not going. You have no right to —

LORRAINE. I'm trying to bring you home, Sal.

SALYER. "Home" is not a basement apartment in St. Paul —

LORRAINE. Garden-level. Garden-level.

SALYER. *(Overlapping.)* — Home is not sleeping on your couch and walking your dog and eating your tuna hotdish —

LORRAINE. *(Overlapping from "eating.")* Okay, so my life's not all FUCKED UP and EXCITING like *yours* —

SALYER. *(Hot.)* You know — okay — I don't get it: I'm thirty-five years old and *now* you *give a shit? Now* you start *parenting?*

LORRAINE. *(To Ben.)* They say the darndest things.

SALYER. I AM NOT A CHILD.

LORRAINE. YOU CAN SAY THAT AGAIN. *(To Ben.)* Only a full-fledged adult could wreck a life the way she's wrecked hers. Can't hold a *job.* Disappears for *months at a time* —

SALYER. *(Overlapping from "job.")* Oh, jesus … *enough, okay?!*

LORRAINE. Lets some man tattoo every inch of her — like she's some kind of damn *pin cushion. (To Salyer.)* God, you can PICK 'EM.

SALYER. *I* can pick 'em?! What about the PARADE OF CLOWNS?! Have you forgotten about them? Or maybe you never knew their names — as long as they'd fill you with whiskey-sevens —

LORRAINE. That's too far, Sal —

SALYER. *(Overlapping.)* — and take off their wedding rings while they *fucked you* —

LORRAINE. *(Ice.)* That is WAY too far —

SALYER. *(Overlapping, to Ben.)* Sweet Mama Lorraine cut a BIT OF A SWATH through the daddies in our town.

LORRAINE. After your father left, I was —

SALYER. After he *"left"*? HE DIDN'T LEAVE! They *took him away* — they *drafted him!*

LORRAINE. It's so easy —

SALYER. I NEVER EVEN MET HIM.

LORRAINE. — So easy to judge, baby — until *you're* the one left behind.

SALYER. I won't let that happen to me.

LORRAINE. Oh, I suppose this "Jeeter" is the answer! Some old hippie — living out of his car —

SALYER. He's not a hippie — he was NEVER A HIPPIE — he's a PROFESSOR — and he's a VET — he's a VIETNAM VET —

LORRAINE. Oh, well — *THAT puts a mother's mind at ease*, let me tell you.

LORRAINE. *(To Ben.)* My little angel and her "Vietnam vet complex" — tell my daughter a war story and *her panties just fall to the ground* —	SALYER. Listen to me — You don't know him —

SALYER. — YOU DON'T KNOW HIM AT ALL.

LORRAINE. Oh, I'm sure he has a *LOT to offer* —

SALYER. Yes, he does.

LORRAINE. WHAT? What has the man ever DONE?!

SALYER. He got me away from *you*. *(Direct hit, just as — Jeeter rushes on, out of breath. Sees Salyer —)*

JEETER. Hey. *(They all just stare at him.)* Where *were you*? *(Salyer turns away, says nothing. Hot.)* I drove off lookin' for you — *the fog thick as shit* — but I just barreled ahead — lookin' *everywhere* —

SALYER. I went for a walk.

JEETER. A *walk?*

SALYER. Yes.

JEETER. You climbed out the bathroom window to *go for a walk?!*

LORRAINE. *(To Jeeter.)* Welcome to my world.

SALYER. *(To Jeeter.)* Let's go for a drive.

JEETER. *What?!*

SALYER. I want to see the fog.

33

LORRAINE. We have a ten A.M. flight out of Modesto —

SALYER. You have a safe trip, Lorraine. Pet the dog for me. *(To Jeeter.)* Let's go.

JEETER. *(A WAY larger explanation is needed here.)* Sal — ?

SALYER. Can we just *GO?* *(And she does just that.)*

JEETER. *(Calling after her.)* SALYER! *(But she's gone. Jeeter stares at Lorraine; stares at Ben.)* This is not us.

BEN. Right.

JEETER. Don't judge us on this. We can do better.

BEN. See you. *(And Jeeter goes. And Lorraine stands there for a long time.)* Isn't there somewhere you need to be?

LORRAINE. Not at all. Lucky you. *(Lorraine plops herself down in a chair.)* Got something to drink?

BEN. I've got coffee.

LORRAINE. I don't *do* coffee. Never did.

BEN. Okay —

LORRAINE. I do whiskey. And I bet you've got some. You seem like the type that'd have some *bad whiskey* on hand — all that Jim and Jack and Johnny crap. *Good* whiskey — just FYI — *good* whiskey does not have a *first name. (Beat.)* Still, if you've got some, okay, sure, twist my arm. *(Ben goes into the trailer, as — Lorraine picks up the little snowy knick-knack ... turns it over ... and watches the orange snow fall.)* So: this "Jeeter"? He was a friend of yours over there?

BEN. *(From trailer.)* We served together, yeah.

LORRAINE. How old were you?

BEN. *(Entering.)* Not very. *(Lorraine nods. Ben brings whiskey and two glasses. Pours.)*

LORRAINE. And this is what? The final "hurrah?"

BEN. Jeeter's here every summer. *(Lorraine smiles. Off her look.)* What?

LORRAINE. Yeah, it's weird. Friends are like furniture. When they get old and worn out, you turn the bad side to the wall; cover the stains with pillows. But damned if you don't *sit on 'em anyway. (Beat.)* With women it gets all hinky and complicated — women "move on" or "grow apart" or "have a falling out." But men — I don't know — men just *change bars. (Lorraine lifts her whiskey, drinks. Pause. Then, it just comes out ...)* I never told her. I never told Sal about her dad. Whenever she asked, I just said he left me for someone else, because, hey — and I don't care how this sounds

34

— that's exactly what it *felt like. (Beat.)* God, we were *kids.* My Daniel ... my Danny was a little boy who got his draft notice. And I was a little girl who couldn't tell him — I put him on that plane and I *never* told him —

BEN. What?

LORRAINE. That I had his baby in my gut and not a clue in the world. *(Pause, drinks.)* Left on a Monday. I got some letters from basic training, saying he was shipping out. Next thing I know the Army is calling — telling me my husband is MIA. *Don't I know it,* I said. My Danny's been MIA since he first got his draft notice. We're eighteen years old and he reads that thing and I watch this ... *fog* ... just ... *cover his face.* And I tell him I love him and that I want to spend my life with him, and that ... *fog* ... just ... *does not lift.* To this very day, I listen to people debate that war and what it *did* and what it *meant* and I just want to SHAKE these idiots and make them understand that that war was NOTHING BUT A VAST GLOBAL CONSPIRACY TO *BREAK MY FUCKING HEART. (Pause, still hard.)* As you can see, I'm *over it.* All in the past. Doesn't bother me at all.

BEN. He didn't make it home?

LORRAINE. Showed up on the Wall. Still MIA. *God — the lengths a man will go to get away from a woman. (Beat.)* But then that tattoo freak had to take Sal to the Wall. And she sees Danny's name. And she comes home and stands in my kitchen demanding the "truth" — and I tell her that no one in their right mind wants the damn "truth" — and then oh boy did we ever have ourselves a good old-fashioned *plate-smasher. (Lorraine pours herself some more whiskey.)* Now she thinks her dad's some kind of hero. Not me. I don't think he's MIA. *I don't even think he's dead.* Think he's gonna show up at my door any day now just to twist the dagger — his arm around some skinny young thing with fake tits and a perm that could catch meat. Or maybe he'll just drive past and *wave* — on his way to play a round of golf with that fucker who ran the war — what was his name? — the man with all those *regrets* and all that *anguish* and if you FORK OUT THIRTY BUCKS FOR HIS BOOK HE'LL TELL YOU ALL ABOUT IT —

BEN. *(Rising to the fight.)* McNamara. Robert McNamara.

LORRAINE. I read that book —

BEN. I read that book, too —

LORRAINE. *(Overlapping.)* — I read that book because somebody told me there was an APOLOGY in there — and *oh, baby* did I ever NEED ONE OF THOSE. I needed THAT MAN — I needed *SOME MAN SOMEWHERE* TO JUST SAY THE WORDS: "I'M SORRY." *(Beat.)* Never. Never once. Three hundred damn pages ... *nothing. (Silence.)*

BEN. *(Simple, strong.)* He's a great man. *(Lorraine gives him a long, hard look.)* A great man put in a tragic position.

LORRAINE. You know, when you're drinkin' someone's whiskey it's awful hard to slap 'em across the face — but *I just might have to do that.*

BEN. *(With a fierce pride.)* I not only bought that book — I went to hear him speak. And I had him sign that book for my dad. "That man" — my dad would say — "that man is what *a man oughta be.*" Powerful and efficient; crunching numbers like a machine. And *always a plan* — my dad would say — *he always had a plan* — that was the thing about McNamara, the thing that set him apart: HE HAD A *PLAN.*

LORRAINE. *(Hot.)* Yes, we certainly know *that,* don't we? —

BEN. If you'd just look at the facts —

LORRAINE. Too bad *running the war* was little different than *running Ford Motor* —

BEN. That has nothing to do with —

LORRAINE. Too bad the numbers *crunched* a little harder —

BEN. Robert McNamara was the *first person* — *(She's on her feet now.)*

LORRAINE. You tell my daughter about THE PLAN, okay?!

BEN. — The FIRST PERSON to grasp the REALITY of American involvement in Vietnam.

LORRAINE. *(Overlapping from "American.")* Tell her about that GREAT MAN and HIS PLAN FOR *MY DANNY* — 'cause she's NEVER GONNA HEAR THAT FROM ME. *(And Lorraine throws her drink in Ben's face, and marches off, just as — the Young Soldier enters, with purpose — his dialogue immediate. The persistent drone of helicopters is heard, under:)*

THE YOUNG SOLDIER. *(With force.)* May, 1962. Quote: "There is no plan for introducing combat forces in South Vietnam."

BEN. *(Immediate, wheels on the Young Soldier.)* Yes — that's true. *(The Young Soldier goes to the wash basin — lifts another bucket of water — and pours it into the basin, as before.)*

THE YOUNG SOLDIER. May, 1964 — with *sixteen thousand*

troops in country: "Excellent progress has been made — but additional personnel might be necessary."

BEN. *(Strong, proud.)* Yes — these are my statements on the war —

THE YOUNG SOLDIER. November, 1965 — with *one hundred and forty-five thousand troops in country:*

BEN. Is that your point?!

THE YOUNG SOLDIER. "My most vivid impression is that we have stopped losing the war."

BEN. And YES, they are statements of *fact.*

THE YOUNG SOLDIER. October, 1966 — with *three hundred thirty-one thousand troops in country:*

THE YOUNG SOLDIER.

"I see no reason to expect any significant increase in the level of operations in South Vietnam."	BEN. *(Along with him.)* — any significant increase in the level of operations in South Vietnam —

THE YOUNG SOLDIER. July, 1967 — with *four hundred sixty-six thousand troops in country:*

BEN. *(Explodes, with passion.)* THE VIETNAM WAR IS UNPOPULAR IN THIS COUNTRY. I know that. Believe me: *I know that. (As he speaks: Ben goes to the locker. Yanks the white shirt from its hanger. Brings the shirt to the wash basin — and shoves it down into the water. During the following, he proceeds to wash the ever-living-shit out of that shirt. No soap. No brush. Just brute strength.)* Most Americans do not know how we got where we are, and most are convinced that somehow we should not have gotten in this deeply —

THE YOUNG SOLDIER. Yes, sir, that's —

BEN. *(Overlapping.)* — because the *picture* — the picture of the world's greatest superpower *killing or injuring one thousand noncombatants a week while trying to pound a tiny backward nation into submission on an issue whose merits are hotly disputed —* THAT PICTURE ... is not a *pretty one. (Finished washing the shirt, finished with his outburst: Ben takes a long, deep breath. The helicopter drone is gone — giving way to a low, moaning wind. Ben pulls the wet shirt out of the water ... holds it above the basin ... letting it drip into the water below. After a long moment, he speaks ...)* Where you from, soldier?

THE YOUNG SOLDIER. Northern California, sir.

BEN. As am I.

THE YOUNG SOLDIER. Yes, sir.

BEN. Where?

THE YOUNG SOLDIER. A little town east of Eureka.

BEN. Bayside? Blue Lake?

THE YOUNG SOLDIER. Salyer.

BEN. *(Pause.)* Salyer, California. On the river, isn't it?

THE YOUNG SOLDIER. Yes, sir. *(Pause. Ben now begins to wring the water from the shirt with his hands.)* Do you know it, sir?

BEN. What I remember … is the *fog*. A man could walk out into that fog … and he could just … *disappear. (Beat, more quietly.)* Wouldn't that be something? *(A final jet strafes the sky, as — the lights rush to black.)*

End of Act One

ACT TWO

Through the Fog

Music plays in the darkness: It's probably something like the Stones' "Sympathy for the Devil." *

Lights rise as the song is ending, revealing —

Jeeter sitting in the yard.

Ben comes out of the trailer. In one hand he has a coffee pot and a couple mugs. In the other hand he has six plain cake donuts skewered on the tire iron we saw earlier.

Ben pours Jeeter some coffee. Jeeter takes a sip.

BEN. Bad enough for you?
JEETER. *(Re: the coffee.)* Bad as ever.
BEN. Eat up. *(And Ben tilts the tire iron so that a few of the donuts fall into Jeeter's waiting hand. Nice. Ben sits with his own coffee and his own donuts and the morning has attained a rugged sort of order. Chewing. Sipping. Birds in the damn trees. The white shirt hangs on the line. Dry as dust now.)*
JEETER. I ever tell you what Sammy did that time? When we got back to the world, we took all the money we'd been sending home — the money our parents put into little savings accounts so we could go to college and meet virgins — and me and Sammy decided: "Fuck it, let's buy shit." So I went out and bought a new turntable — got it all set up — had the new Fleetwood Mac record — and NO, NOT THAT FLEETWOOD MAC —
BEN. Yeah, Jeet, I know.
JEETER. *(This is a MAJOR point.)* Everybody — god, especially

* See Special Note on Songs and Recordings on copyright page.

my students — think I'm talking about LATER FLEETWOOD MAC when those two chicks joined up and that band went — like the rest of this great country — TOTALLY TO SHIT.

BEN. And also went platinum.

JEETER. Point taken — but I'm talking EARLY MAC — when that group BELONGED to Peter Green — I'm talking about the third album:

BEN. *Then Play On.*

JEETER. *Then Play On.* Oh, *god,* that album:

BEN. A "masterpiece."

JEETER. A masterpiece. That band — AGAIN, BEFORE THOSE SAD-EYED GIRLS WITH ALL THEIR FEATHERS AND MASCARA SLEPT THEIR WAY INTO THAT BAND — and, okay, I mean who can really *blame* those guys — sometimes the *little head* does the thinking for the *big head: love,* man, the weapon of mass *distraction* —

BEN. And the point is — ?

JEETER. I had just put that album (I think it was that, maybe not, whatever) — just had put that album on my new turntable and stepped out of the room — and Sammy took the record off and *put a little donut on there.* You know — he put the spindle up through the —

BEN. Yeah, Jeet, I think I get it.

JEETER. And I come back into the room and say: Sammy, what happened to the music?

BEN. *(Flatly.)* And you look and see that donut.

JEETER. Just spinning around and around.

BEN. It would do that, yeah.

JEETER. *Where the record was supposed to be.*

BEN. *I get the picture.*

JEETER. And the thing I keep wondering —

BEN. Uh-huh.

JEETER. — is how long are you gonna let me make up stories before you *tell me what you think?!* *(Quick beat. Ben stares at him.)*

BEN. What?

JEETER. DO YOU LIKE HER? *(Before Ben can respond.)* GOD! One hour! I've been here one entire hour and you don't bring it up! I ask so very little of you — the crumbs from the table of your trailer park life — and *EVEN THAT* I have to BLEED OUT OF YOU. *(More silence. Ben takes this opportunity to finish his donut. Finally ...)*

BEN. She's nice.

JEETER. *(Complete mood change.)* You think?

BEN. Yeah. I mean, she's kind of ...

JEETER. What?

BEN. Kinda young.

JEETER. The hell does that mean?

BEN. What's it *mean?*

JEETER. Yes — what am I to *take from that?*

BEN. From me saying she's young?

JEETER. Yes.

BEN. Well, by saying "she's young" I obviously mean: She's *tall.*

JEETER. She's thirty-five years old!

BEN. Compared to *us,* though, she's sort of —

JEETER. She's not young, Ben —

BEN. Okay.

JEETER. — She's *old.*

BEN. Okay: She's OLD.

JEETER. She's, like, twenty years older than most the girls I date at school.

BEN. I, like, bet she is.

JEETER. Jesus —

BEN. You asked me what I thought and —

JEETER. And I told you WHAT TO SAY and you can't even grant me THAT!

BEN. MARRY THAT GIRL. Okay. There. *Happy now?* Marry that girl and get the fuck out of here.

JEETER. Is this about the money?

BEN. What?!

JEETER. The five hundred bucks. C'mon —

BEN. Why would this be about —

JEETER. I mean, hey — *we're down to it now* — so at least do me the favor of coming clean about the money.

BEN. You want me to COME CLEAN?

JEETER. Yes, I do.

BEN. Come clean about THE MONEY *YOU OWE ME?*

JEETER. That's what I want.

BEN. Okay —

JEETER. Good —

BEN. WHERE'S MY FUCKING MONEY?!

JEETER. *(Simply.)* I don't have it. *(Ben stares at him in hard, deep, utter disbe-fucking-lief.)* I'm a little short this semester. That so'west trip really set me back.

BEN. It's been *five years,* Jeet.

JEETER. Don't I know it. And it eats at me. It does. Thanks for understanding.

BEN. I don't.

JEETER. Okay.

BEN. I don't understand at all.

JEETER. Okay.

BEN. I don't even WANT the money, Jeet. Forget about the money.

JEETER. *(Smiles.)* Okay, great.

BEN. I just thought you might *bring it up* someday. Five years I've been waiting for you to *make mention of it* — so I could say: "Hey, forget about it. Forget about the money."

JEETER. I *brought* it up.

BEN. Yeah, but —

JEETER. Just this second. It was *brought up.*

BEN. Jeet —

JEETER. And you said: "Forget about it." So, there: It was brought up and you came clean and got everything you wanted, am I right? *(There is a silence here. And something inside Ben just backs away.)*

BEN. Yeah. You're right. *(Another very long silence. God, where did it go? The ease.)*

JEETER. Okay. I'll do it. I'll ask her tonight. Before she gets wise to me, huh?!

BEN. Right.

JEETER. "There is no act so devastating as a true change of heart." *(Pause.)* You know who said that? Your dad said that. He said that to me. *(Ben just stares at him. Increasingly upbeat and nervous:)* So: okay: I'll ask her tonight. Think she'll have me? *(Off Ben's look.)* Yeah, I don't know either. That's why I saved the story. I haven't used the story, yet. *(Off Ben's look.)* My Dylan story.

BEN. Oh, right.

JEETER. *Nineteen sixty-one. Me and Bob.*

BEN. Got it.

JEETER. My Dylan story has never failed me. But with Salyer, I saved it, you know? — because, I didn't need it —

BEN. Well —

JEETER. Not till now.

BEN. — good luck.

JEETER. Thanks. And, hey — I can tell you now. I can tell you about her wearin' all those clothes.

BEN. She told me.

JEETER. No, she didn't.

BEN. Okay.

JEETER. No way would she tell you.

BEN. Okay, then.

JEETER. *About the tattoos?*

BEN. Uh-huh.

JEETER. She *told you?*

BEN. Pretty sure, yeah.

JEETER. Okay. Great. So: There's *that.* See: There's *that* to deal with. She waits TEN DAYS to tell *ME,* but BOOM — SHE MEETS *YOU* and OUT IT COMES.

BEN. *(So VERY done with this.)* Who cares, Jeet? — what's the big —

JEETER. Did she SHOW THEM TO YOU?

BEN. No.

JEETER. Okay. Well. See — that's the thing: I haven't seen 'em. *Nobody's* seen them. She keeps 'em hidden all the time —

BEN. *Got it —*

JEETER. Even in bed — making love to her — she keeps 'em covered — the lights out, the room dark — but one night, Ben, I wake up and I can't stand it any more. She's dead asleep next to me — gloves, long sleeves, the whole deal — and I'm just — there's just this — I gotta just DO THIS — I gotta just do this THING, you know? So, I sit up. I get my flashlight out of my pack. And real slowly and real gently — because, I mean, I am *scared,* Ben, I am shaking like a drunk at Betty Ford — and so real easy-like I pull back the sleeve of her shirt, just an inch or so ... and I shine my light ... and there on her arm I see a tattoo. *(Beat.)* And it is a *name.* It is a *man's* name. And it is not MY NAME — oh, no. And I am pulling back that sleeve another inch — and there is *another name. Another man's name,* Ben. Another man who is NOT ME. And then I get it: *These are the guys she's left behind. (Beat.)* And right away I pull her sleeve down and put my flashlight away — 'cause I don't want to *know* — I don't want to know how many *guys like me* she's left in her wake. I just know that, come what may: I do *not want to end up on that arm. (There, that's out. If you're Jeeter, you're awaiting something from Ben that might move the ship out of this murky water. Instead:)*

43

BEN. *(Re: the trailer.)* What the hell's she doing in there?

JEETER. Making a call.

BEN. Maybe she went for another "walk." *(A beat. Then, Jeeter suddenly stares at the trailer. Realizes: She did it again.)*

JEETER. SALYER?! *(Jeeter rushes toward the trailer door, just as — Salyer casually steps out.)*

SALYER. Yes?

JEETER. You're here.

SALYER. Yes.

JEETER. You didn't climb out the window.

SALYER. Why would I do that? *(He stares at her. It gets real simple. He loves this woman. Calls into the yard:)* Morning. *(Ben just nods.)*

JEETER. Hey — tonight?

SALYER. Hey — yeah?

JEETER. I've got plans for us. Just you and me. Later tonight. Okay?

SALYER. Sure.

JEETER. It's not a concert.

SALYER. Good.

JEETER. And then tomorrow we'll hit the road. Okay?

SALYER. Sure.

JEETER. *Okay?*

SALYER. *(Now, a smile.)* Okay already. *(He kisses her. She holds him, looks in his eyes.)* Do me a favor?

JEETER. Anything —

SALYER. Go find my mother.

JEETER. — but *that.*

SALYER. C'mon, please —

JEETER. I thought we were *running* from your mother.

SALYER. She's in Modesto. About to get on a plane.

JEETER. This is a *good* thing.

SALYER. Just go get her. Get her and bring her back.

JEETER. *Why?!*

SALYER. There's something I need her to see. *(Jeeter stares at Salyer — and gets only her sweet eyes in return. He caves.)*

JEETER. Okay, listen —

SALYER. Tonight.

JEETER. Yes.

SALYER. Just you and me.

JEETER. A night you won't forget. *(Salyer kisses him. Then, Jeeter gets his backpack and prepares to go. To Ben, explaining:)* She doesn't drive. *(Ben nods.)* That's why she needs me to —

SALYER. *(Kindly.)* Thank you, Jeeter.

JEETER. Sure. *(Lost beat.)* Okay. *(Lost beat #2.)* I'm off. *(Lost beat #3.)* I'm just no-doubt *off. (And he is. Silence.)*

BEN. It's three hours.

SALYER. Hmm?

BEN. To Modesto and back.

SALYER. Well, let's hope you're interesting. *(Ben moves away, sits. Sal continues to stand in the yard. Morning pushes on.)* What's this surprise of his? *(Ben's look says: Oh, no you don't.)* You don't know? *(Ben looks away, sips coffee. Simple, definitive:)* Yeah. You know. You know it all. *(Salyer moves closer to Ben than he expects. Sits. Stares at him.)* So ... real busy day, huh? Guess there's nothing that needs to be built. Not *fixed,* mind you — god forbid something in this world actually gets *fixed. (He stares at her, then stands —)*

BEN. Okay: This has been a *lot* of fun. Thank you — *(And starts to leave —)*

SALYER. You know, I'm a little *cold.* Could I borrow a jacket?

BEN. There's a blanket there — *(But Salyer is not listening. She is moving to the military locker.)*

SALYER. Maybe this black one in here — do you mind? I think this will do the trick. It was your dad's, right? And maybe I'll stand up here — give a little speech — answer a few questions. Would that be okay? *(Salyer is wearing the black coat.)*

BEN. *(Angry.)* Listen to me —

SALYER. *Do you believe in ghosts, Ben?* Yeah — me neither — but they keep *turning up now,* don't they?

BEN. This is none of your business —

SALYER. *(Overlapping.)* You know *exactly* what I'm talking about: Who was that soldier standing in this yard?!

BEN. I have no idea.

SALYER. God, you're worse than Lorraine. The truth has to be *shaken* out of you people. I would never have known, you know — about my dad — *my own dad* — she would *never have told me.* But I'm dating this tattoo guy and we're in D.C. and he says: I want to show you the greatest tattoo in the world. It covers the entire body of a woman. A woman carved out of black granite — lying on her side — her belly exposed — her back pushing hard against the earth. And tattooed on this great, black, granite woman: *names.*

Names that cover *every square inch of her. (Pause.)* And so we go to the Wall. And there he is. There's my dad — his name staring right at me. *(Pause.)* And I don't want to leave him. I want to bring that name home and shove it in Lorraine's face and make her see it once and for all. And some nice park ranger is trying to hand me some paper and a pencil — *you can do an etching of the name,* he's saying — but I don't want a piece of paper — no — I know what I want now — I know *exactly* what I want: I want that *name.* I want *all* those names. *(Pause.)* And so I take my boyfriend home. And I take off my clothes. And he goes to work. *(Long silence, during which: Ben approaches Salyer from behind. We think he might be about to embrace her ... but, instead, he reaches over her shoulders and slowly removes the black coat from her body. Remains standing right behind her. She turns to him. A charged moment; eye to eye. Quiet:)* You don't talk about it, do you? Not like Jeeter.

BEN. *That's* what you want? You get me alone and sit real close to me with all those clothes on and that's what you really want to do? — *Talk about the war?*

SALYER. Yeah, maybe I do.

BEN. *(Moving away.)* I think if McLellan had moved his troops when Lincoln asked, the South could have been crushed years earlier and the nation spared the slaughter at Antietam. *(Beat.) That* was a war. Vietnam was a "tactical exercise" — a prolonged one, as it turned out — designed to bring about a change of regime in a distant, critically situated country. Period.

SALYER. Yeah, I read that. In Jeeter's book. He quotes your dad saying that.

BEN. Jeeter did *not* know my dad.

SALYER. Then why was he was back in Michigan *twice a month* for, what? — almost a *year?* Your dad turned your old room into Jeeter's *office,* for god's sake. *(This lands. Ben says nothing.)* There's still this debate about the title: They want him to call it *Change of Heart* — but Jeeter wants to have the word "ghost" in the title. He keeps saying: "Gotta be a ghost in there somewhere." I told him: When a publisher gives you a *six-figure advance,* they get to call it whatever they want. *(Beat.)* Quite the deal, huh? What's Jeeter gonna do with all that money? *(Again: Ben says nothing.)* He told you this, right?

BEN. *(No, none of it.)* Oh, yeah. *(Silence. The tone shifts.)*

SALYER. So ... what else don't you talk about? Would you like to

NOT talk about the sixties? I'd like that a *lot* — if we could *not do that*. You can *have it,* okay? — take the whole fucking decade — I don't want it — I'm sick of it and glad I missed it and, trust me: You can't name *one thing* I wish I'd seen or done during the whole over-blown, over-hyped, over-sold *mess. (He's looking at her now. She meets his gaze, challenging.)*

BEN. *(An edge to his voice.)* You're right. *Take it.* Throw it away. I won't miss it. *(Pause.)* Nineteen sixty-one. It's yours. Take it. New York City. I'm young and stupid and cold and eager and hungry and fifteen years old. You can take that, too. I don't want it. There's a shop in the Village. Izzy Young's Folklore Center. You don't have to take that — it's already long gone. I walk into the back room. And a kid my age is playin' a guitar. He's singin' about. A house. In New Orleans. And then he starts blowin' on a harp. And that's what I can't forget. And that's what you *can't* take — 'cause it's not mine to give you. You can't take away the look on that kid's face while he wrestles with that harp. Like he and that harp are fighting each other for the *last known breath on earth. (Pause.)* Just a scrawny kid from Minnesota. Did pretty well for himself. A little over-blown —

SALYER. You mean Dylan.

BEN. Over-hyped —

SALYER. You mean *Bob Dylan.*

BEN. Over-sold. But hey, there it is.

SALYER. No way. *(Ben shrugs. Moves away. Picks up the snowy knick-knack. Salyer considers the story.)* There's *no way.*

BEN. Suit yourself.

SALYER. How many people were in that room?

BEN. About six. You hungry?

SALYER. Six people.

BEN. Like I said —

SALYER. And you.

BEN. Take it —

SALYER. *And Dylan?*

BEN. — I don't want it. *(Ben tips the little snowy knick-knack over. Watches the orange "snow" fall.)*

SALYER. Does Jeeter know this?

BEN. Oh, yeah. *(Beat.)* See: You didn't miss a thing. *(And, saying this, he tosses the paperweight across the yard and BAM: into the dumpster, as —*

Music plays: something nice and loud like "Fresh Garbage" by Spirit, continuing through the following:*

Salyer leaves the yard — and Ben settles into his chair once again, staring into the distance, as —

Lights shift from morning to midnight, moonlight flooding the yard once again, as now —

Lorraine, Jeeter and Salyer spill into the yard. Eventually, they will claim some chairs around the fire; their faces lit by its glow. They are drinking beer. Munching on chips. No doubt sharing a joint. They're loud. And they're lit. But they're only as drunk as you need them to be; just enough to make them brash and bold.)

JEETER. But but but but but but listen: That's what she does!

LORRAINE. Noooooooooo!   SALYER. It is a such a scam.

JEETER. It Is What She DOES.

LORRAINE. You're making this up.

JEETER. Sal was there — ask her — am I making this up?

SALYER. I wish you were.   BEN. Who is this person?

JEETER. She's a *PSYCHIC.*

LORRAINE. And you went there *on purpose?*

JEETER. She's *highly regarded.* Her website gets like two hundred hits an hour —

LORRAINE. *(Overlapping from "two hundred.")* And what? — you get there and she says: "Hi, my name is —

JEETER. Raven.   SALYER. *"Raven."*

(Sal is laughing now. Lorraine is combatively curious.)

LORRAINE. — and I'll be your *psychic* for the evening —

JEETER. You have a very bad attitude about this —

LORRAINE. *(Overlapping from "attitude.")* And I'm gonna tell your future by *smelling your urine* — (Gross reaction from Ben and Sal.) So: Here's a bowl. GO PEE IN IT. *(Sal and Lorraine have a good laugh at this — and Ben perhaps joins them.)*

JEETER. Hey — laugh — that's fine — DENY the mystery — DENY the darkness — DENY the *divinity within you* —

LORRAINE. Oh, I love this: SALYER. They don't care, Mr. More Spiritual Than Thou.   Jeeter — just let it go —

JEETER. DENY THE UNSEEN AT YOUR PERIL!

BEN. Hey, Jeet —

JEETER. Because, hey, when the Cosmic Push Comes to Shove:

---

* See Special Note on Songs and Recordings on copyright page.

I'm gonna be *basking in light* somewhere and you people — you *doubters*, you *cold-hard-proof-needers* — you're gonna be nothin' but DUST —
BEN. Jeet —
JEETER. COMPOST —
BEN. JEET —
JEETER. VULTURE PATÉ —
BEN. GET A LIFE!
JEETER. GET AN *AFTER*LIFE! *(And Salyer and Jeeter crack up again — holding each other, maybe falling to the ground, arm in arm. Ben is not laughing.)*
SALYER. *(To Ben.)* You got any music?
JEETER. No, he does NOT —
BEN. Yes, I do —
JEETER. He's got *CDs.*
BEN. Oh, god.   SALYER. So, what?
JEETER. So WHAT?! *CDs are not music.*
BEN. *(To Sal, with a laugh.)* He's got this *thing* — don't ask —
JEETER. *(Overlapping.)* I'm not gonna do it. I'm not gonna listen to perfectly good music get whitewashed and packaged and put on a *shiny little pancake.*
LORRAINE. This just in: *Time Passes.*
BEN. *(Saluting.)* He's an All   SALYER. Look — nobody
Vinyl Man. *Vinyl Uber Alles.*   cares, okay? — nobody
                                          cares about —
JEETER. *(Overlapping.)* Yeah — you go ahead — put your *CD* in its little *tray* — and watch it vanish inside like a corpse at the morgue — and you crank up the Stones — and you listen to that nasty guitar chord right before the chorus of "Brown Sugar" — *"you should have heard her just around midnight"* — *(Imitates the famous chord.)* — and that great chord on a CD sounds like fuckin' muzak — like bad sex in a cold room with a thick condom. BUT: You play that same song on *vinyl* — on a good ol' garage sale turntable — and when Keith hits that chord — *(Imitates chord again.)* — your hands will shake for a fucking WEEK. (Salyer has lift-ed the JUST STOP sign which has been laying nearby. She now holds it right in front of Jeeter's face.) I got it. (Raise his arms, surrenders.) I hear you. (Smiles, to Ben.) See that: The sign works. (Lorraine pro-duces a flask from her purse.)
LORRAINE. *(To Ben.)* Hey, Mister McNamara — get us some

49

glasses.

BEN. What did you call me?

LORRAINE. Mister God Bless The Military Republican Man —

JEETER. Ben's not a Republican.

BEN. You don't know that. *(Ben stands and heads inside. Jeeter is staring at Salyer.)*

LORRAINE. *God, I wish I was.* I've tried for years. But something always gets in the way: tolerance, compassion, human decency —

SALYER. Okay, Lorraine, we get it.

JEETER. I love this woman. I love your daughter, Lorraine.

LORRAINE. *(Flat.)* Uh-huh.

JEETER. And I know just what you're thinking.

LORRAINE. Then why are you still here? *(Jeeter just laughs this off, god love him.)*

SALYER. *(Wistfully.)* "Black Magic Woman." *(To Lorraine.)* Remember that?

LORRAINE. Santana.

SALYER. You had that great album —

LORRAINE. I'm *such* a good mother.

SALYER. — and every Friday night, I had to hide it under my bed.

LORRAINE. Oh, *must we* go into this?

SALYER. Yes, I think we *must. (Ben arrives with some clean glasses.) (To Ben and Jeeter.)* I grew up in a NEVER-ENDING GARAGE SALE.

LORRAINE. *(Weary.)* God — here it comes.

SALYER. *(Overlapping.)* Every Friday night Lorraine would haul everything we owned out onto the lawn — and every Monday she'd *haul back in whatever didn't sell.*

LORRAINE. And here's the other thing: The money we got from that *crap* is what we *ate with.*

SALYER. So, I spent every Friday night of my childhood hiding all my favorite toys and clothes and records —

LORRAINE. *(Lifting her glass.)* All bow to the Evil Bitch.

SALYER. *(Overlapping.)* — and all weekend I'd watch my stuff be carried away by strangers. I couldn't wait for Monday — just to get away and go to school — but half the time she'd keep me home — just to *keep her company* — *(Salyer is standing behind Lorraine's chair now — stroking her hair.)*

LORRAINE. Which you were very good at.

SALYER. And mix her drinks —

LORRAINE. Which you were not.

SALYER. — And then she'd write the same note to the principal, every time: "Please excuse Salyer's absence. *Death in the family.*"

LORRAINE. Hey, it was *true.*

SALYER. *Twice a week, Mom?* That's an awful lotta "death in the family."

LORRAINE. Well, *that's what it felt like, baby. (Jeeter has been squirming throughout the entire preceding section; he's trying to squelch what he needs to say — but it's killing him.)*

SALYER. *(Seeing Jeeter's actions.)* What?! *(Jeeter shakes his head; buttons his lips.)* WHAT?!

JEETER. *Santana?*

SALYER. You don't like Santana?

LORRAINE. Oh, live in the world —

JEETER. That's NOT Santana.

SALYER. Of course it is.

JEETER. "Black Magic Woman" was written by PETER GREEN. That's a FLEETWOOD MAC SONG. WAY before Santana. But, does anybody know that? — does anyone give a righteous rat's ass?!

LORRAINE. *(Out of the blue.)* I dated Cat Stevens. *(Beat.)* Once. *(Beat.)* Sort of. *(Long silence. They're all staring at her, frozen. Smiles, re: their baffled non-reaction.)* Okay. That still works. *(Another long, lost silence. They drink/smoke. Night deepens. Crickets thrive.)*

JEETER. *(Re: the whiskey.)* God, this is good. Where did you get this?

LORRAINE. My trip to Scotland.

JEETER. Really? Did you go into the remote villages?

LORRAINE. I went into the bars.

JEETER. 'Cause the thing is — when *I* went there —

BEN. Oh, here we go.

SALYER. Is this another *quest?*

JEETER. I went on this pilgrimage — back into these settlements where — to this day — you can still find someone known as the "Sin-Eater." Usually an old man — an outcast — and he's paid to "eat the sins" of the dead. To cleanse them and pave their way into heaven.

SALYER. Jeeter, they really don't want to hear this —

JEETER. The body is placed before the old man. On the chest of the corpse is placed a piece of bread. And the old man is paid to lift the bread off the corpse and eat it … thereby transferring all the sins of the dead to himself. Consuming them forever. And then this old man, this outcast — he turns and walks away into the hills. A man filled with sin. *(Pause.)* If you see that ... if you let yourself really *see that* ... it will *change you* ... *(And this hangs in the air like any late-night story: both impossible and true. Finally ...)*

LORRAINE. I'll tell you about "life-changing moments." One morning you get out of bed and open the fridge and reach for the juice — just like you've done every day of your life ... but on this morning, you watch your hand just shove that juice to the side. And reach past it. And grab a beer. And you crack it open. And you sit in your chair. And that's how your life changes. In stupid little ways. *(Silence. Jeeter lifts his glass.)*

JEETER. Excellent. Just ... excellent.

LORRAINE. Single malt. Eighteen years.

JEETER. *(Quiet.)* Shit, Ben — we killed people younger than this scotch. *(Okay. That happened. Lorraine is staring at Jeeter. It seems very likely that she will say something to make everything much worse — but, instead, she turns her attention to Salyer.)*

LORRAINE. *(Re: Jeeter.)* Loverboy said you'd tell me why I drove all the way back here. *(Flat.)* Not that I'm not having *the time of my life.* (Salyer stares at her for a long time.)*

SALYER. *Cat Stevens?*

LORRAINE. I'm *such* a bad mother.

SALYER. Ben's got you beat, though. *Dylan.* In sixty-one. Before he was even "Dylan." *Six people in the room. (To Jeeter.)* Amazing. Isn't it? *(Jeeter is giving Ben a long hard stare. Ben is not backing down.)*

JEETER. *(Dry.)* Yes. *(Pause.)* Yes, it is. *(An odd, drunken silence.)* Ben's done a lot of amazing things. *(Jeeter looks at Ben — waiting to see if he'll stop him. He gets only Ben's cold, hard stare.)* Has he told you about the three soldiers on a road? This was outside Dak To. *(To Ben.)* More of a path, really. Right? *(No response.)* Ben doesn't mind if I tell this. I'm his best friend in the world, *right?!* *(No response.)* Little red dirt path through the jungle. Three grunts on patrol. They come across a body. Viet Cong soldier. Seventeen, tops. Crispy-crittered by some napalm. But still alive. Some of his face gone. The soldiers spit on the ground. They all three know they gotta put this kid out of his misery. It's just a matter of who's gonna do it. The first soldier steps forward. "Fuck it" — he says — "I'll do it." Lifts his rifle to the kid's head — and then there's screaming. Someone running out of the jungle. An old woman.

Hands in the air. Trying to stop them from doing this to — who? — her son, maybe? The soldiers are trying to shove her away — but this *mama-san* is wailing like a siren — and then she's *on top of her son.* Arms wrapped around him tight. And now the soldiers get it: She doesn't want him saved. She wants to *die with him.* Now, the second soldier steps forward — tries to pull the woman off her son, but she's hangin' on for dear life — back and forth they roll — this sobbing mass rolling up and down the road — the second soldier is *screaming* at the old woman: "*DIDI MAU, DIDI MAU*"— trying to wrench them apart — and *crying* — now he's *crying* — the second soldier is shaking and crying *and he still can't pry this mother from her son.* The third soldier steps forward, cigarette in his mouth. He lifts his rifle. Aims it at the woman's leg. Fires. Her leg shatters. Aims at the other leg. Fires. She right away goes into shock — eyes rolling back in her head — still clutching her son. The third soldier turns to the others. "She wants to die with him. Let her die with him." And he walks on. (*Long silence. Even Jeeter keeps staring front — somehow still "looking at" the story after he's told it. Finally, Salyer turns to Ben.*)
SALYER. (*Quietly, to Ben.*) That happened to you?
JEETER. You bet it did. And when you ask him which soldier he was — he'll never tell. And I'll never tell — 'cause I would never do that to a *friend.*
BEN. (*Ice.*) That's enough, Jeet —
JEETER. Told his dad, though. Wrote him a letter. Thought his dad would *understand.* His dad — the McNamara-Man; the Win-At-Any-Cost-Man. But, when he got that letter, do you know what his father did? (*Salyer and Lorraine each look to Ben for the answer.*) Don't look at Ben. He doesn't know. His dad never told him this. (*Looks at Ben.*) Am I *right?!* (*Ben just stares at him: Go ahead, you fuck, finish it.*) His dad took a red marker. And he wrote four words at the top of that letter: WHAT. IS. THE. PLAN? And he put that letter in an envelope — and he addressed it to the Secretary of Defense, his former boss, the honorable Robert S. McNamara. And that's how I found it. Lying in a pile of papers — in a basement — in Michigan. It was never sent. And right next to that letter, I found *a signed copy of McNamara's book* — with the same four words written at the top: WHAT. IS. THE. PLAN?
BEN. (*Sharp.*) They gave you six figures for that story? You must have told 'em some *whoppers,* old buddy.
JEETER. (*Not backing down.*) Nothing that's not true.

BEN. Sneaking behind my back — stalking my old man —

JEETER. That's not what I did —

BEN. You shameless, lying, little *fuck* —

JEETER. *(Overlapping.)* I went there to mend fences for you, *old buddy.*

BEN. *Bullshit* —

JEETER. I went there because *he wanted to talk,* Ben — but where the hell were you? Holed up in your trailer — wasting away in the middle of nowhere —

BEN. *(Overlapping.)* You had no right to —

JEETER. So: He talked to *me.* It just poured out of him, okay?!

BEN. Listen to me —

JEETER. For days on end he'd talk and *none of it was for me* — don't you think I know that?! — it was for YOU — it was ALL FOR YOU!

SALYER. Jeeter — stop it —

JEETER. *(Overlapping.)* He was *haunted,* Ben. He saw McNamara walking through his house! — giving briefings in his damn *yard!*

BEN. Don't talk like you *knew him,* okay?! You didn't know the *first thing* about my dad —

JEETER. I know he had a *change of heart — and you never forgave him for that. (This lands.)* He *wrote you,* he *called you,* he *came here* and *pounded on this door* — but you WOULD NOT SEE HIM! *God* — the *DENIAL* — you and McNamara *DESERVE EACH OTHER.*

BEN. And that's *another person* you don't know the first thing about!

JEETER. I TEACH THIS, BEN.

BEN. You *"TEACH THIS"*? You don't fucking *teach this* — you *USE this.* You haul out the sixties —

SALYER. *(Sharp.)* Oh — put the sixties to bed!

LORRAINE. *(To Salyer.)* Sorry, babe: It's all we GOT.

BEN. — You haul out the war —

BEN. — and you drape yourself in the whole lousy mess and you say: LOOK AT ME! I WAS THERE! Must be a great way to get in the *pants of the coeds.*

JEETER. OKAY: BOMBS AWAY! *There's* the McNamara we KNOW AND LOVE!

BEN. He did NOT advocate the bombing —

JEETER. Oh, yeah — there's my boy —

BEN. In public, he had to appear strong, had to stand behind his President —

JEETER. Oh, yeah, give it to me now —

BEN. But *behind the scenes*, on *the inside* —

JEETER. Gimme that *inside stuff*—

BEN. He was urging *restraint* — trying to *scale it back* —

JEETER. Oh, *right* —

BEN. And when that didn't work — when that wouldn't sway the hawks who wanted to *bomb the North into oblivion* — I went PUBLIC —

JEETER. *Who* did?

BEN. I went before the committee and I told them —

JEETER. *Who* told them?!

BEN. *I did. I told them. (Fierce, crying out.)* I am the Secretary of Defense and I am responsible for these lives! — And I believe that a new air campaign against the North would not only be futile — it would involve *risks to our nation that I am unable to recommend.*

JEETER. *(Applauding.)* Oh, BRAVO.

BEN. *(Overlapping.)* The war in Vietnam is acquiring a *momentum of its own that MUST BE STOPPED. (Jeeter gets right in Ben's face —)*

JEETER. And you reached this conclusion as early as nineteen sixty-FIVE, *isn't that true?* —

BEN. I believe that it —

JEETER. *(Overlapping.)* — And YET: You remained in your position till November of sixty-*SEVEN* — TWO YEARS after you determined *the war could not be won.* And *never* in those two years did you *come forward. Never* did you publicly state *your strong opposition to the war* — ISN'T THAT TRUE?! *(There is no response. They are eye to eye. Breathing hard. Quiet, taut:)* And in *those two years alone:* What was the *body count? (Beat.)* What were the *names? (Ben does not look away; but no answer comes. A hard whisper:)* Yeah. That's what I thought. *(And now ... Jeeter turns ... and leaves. Not into the trailer — towards his van. The road. Away. Silence. No one moves. Finally: Lorraine turns to Ben.)*

LORRAINE. *(Quiet, direct.)* You know what? ... I respect that the man wanted to apologize. I really do. But where I come from, when you're sorry you don't *write a book.* You don't go on *TV.* This is what you do: You get the list of names. And next to those names, an address or a phone number. And you start with "A." And you knock on that door. Dial that number. And when someone answers, you tell them who you are. And what you did. And you say you're sorry. Then you move on. Till you're done. Till you've accounted for the last of those boys. *(Pause.)* And if it takes the rest of your life, then it takes the rest of your life. *(Lorraine exits, into the trailer, as — Distant helicopters are heard, and — The Young Soldier appears in the yard. Ben does not turn to face him. From across the yard: Salyer sees him, too.)*

THE YOUNG SOLDIER. Mr. Secretary. The ceremony will begin shortly. The President will present you with the Medal of Freedom in the East Room, and you'll be asked to make some departing remarks. *(Salyer calls into the trailer —)*

SALYER. *(Quiet, urgent.)* Mom ... come here ...

THE YOUNG SOLDIER. Have you prepared your remarks, sir? *(Now: Ben turns to the Young Soldier, approaches him.)*

BEN. *(Quiet, hoarse.)* Who were you with?

THE YOUNG SOLDIER. Pardon me, sir?

BEN. What division?

THE YOUNG SOLDIER. 1st Infantry.

BEN. The Big Red One.

THE YOUNG SOLDIER. Yes, sir.

BEN. Rank?

THE YOUNG SOLDIER. Specialist.

BEN. Grade?

THE YOUNG SOLDIER. Four.

BEN. Have you filed your report?

THE YOUNG SOLDIER. No, sir.

BEN. Would you care to do that now — tonight?

THE YOUNG SOLDIER. *(Pause.)* Yes, sir. *(Ben nods. Waits. The Young Soldier turns and faces front.)*

BEN. *(Evenly, not fast.)* Location of Action.

THE YOUNG SOLDIER. Kontum Province.

BEN. Mission.

THE YOUNG SOLDIER. Secure and hold area. Conduct reconnaissance in force, within assigned area of operations.

BEN. Weather.

THE YOUNG SOLDIER. Early morning fog. Light rain, variable winds. Temperature: 96 degrees.

BEN. Terrain.

THE YOUNG SOLDIER. Mountainous to open plains.

BEN. Time.

THE YOUNG SOLDIER. Oh six-twenty hours.

BEN. Action.

THE YOUNG SOLDIER. Armored personnel carrier hit by B-40 rocket and destroyed. Eight wounded; one killed in action.

BEN. List of KIA.

THE YOUNG SOLDIER. Daniel Edward Landon.

BEN. Service number.

THE YOUNG SOLDIER. 325687509.

BEN. Age.

THE YOUNG SOLDIER. Nineteen.

BEN. Home.

THE YOUNG SOLDIER. Salyer, California.

BEN. Religion.

THE YOUNG SOLDIER. Protestant.

BEN. Marital status.

THE YOUNG SOLDIER. Married.

BEN. Children.

THE YOUNG SOLDIER. None.

BEN. Died.

THE YOUNG SOLDIER. Kontum Province, South Vietnam, 29 August 1967. *(Silence. Then ... the Young Soldier reaches into his shirt and pulls out his dog tags. He yanks one of the dog tags [on its own small chain] away from the other ... turns ... and hands this dog tag to Ben, placing it in Ben's open palm. Ben stares at the dog tag. Turns. Moves away — across the yard, toward the military locker, as — Salyer steps slowly towards the Young Soldier.)*

SALYER. *(Quietly.)* Hi. *(The Young Soldier looks right at her — not moving.)* Mom still makes your coffee. To this day, she makes one cup every morning. Sets it on the table. Never touches it. Says she just likes the smell. But it's for you. I know it's for you. *(The Young Soldier continues to stare at her, as — Lorraine emerges from the trailer — her back to the Young Soldier — looking at Salyer. Pleading now:)* Say something. Please ... *(He does not. She waits. He keeps staring at her.)*

LORRAINE. Sal.

SALYER. Lorraine. He's here.

LORRAINE. Go to bed, honey. You're drunk.

SALYER. He's right here. Just come over here. Come and *look*. *(Lorraine moves to her — looks hard into her face —)*

LORRAINE. Is this about your dad, Sal? Are we doing this again?

SALYER. *Say* something. He's *right here* —

LORRAINE. He's your hero, is that it? The man who never disappointed you. Here's the thing, baby: They die when they're still boys, they don't have time to hurt you. But he would have. He'd of hurt me. And I'd have hurt him. And we'd have disappointed you. And grown old. And wished to hell that we were kids again. *(And now — as Lorraine turns to go — she stops. And she sees him. There is no doubt about it. She sees him. The Young Soldier even takes a step towards her — meeting her gaze. Finally ... still staring at the Young Soldier ... Lorraine speaks to Salyer — simply:)* There's no one here, baby. *(And she goes into the trailer, as —)*

SALYER. *(From her gut.) Please* — you have to *say something ...* *(But the Young Soldier simply stares at her. Now: Fighting tears, Salyer begins to take off the layers of clothing which cover her torso — her coat, sweater, scarf, shirt, etc. — until, turning to face the Young Soldier, we glimpse her entire, naked back. And there we see: tattoos — the names — the names from the Wall, hundreds of them, which cover every inch of her back and neck and arms. Then: Salyer points to a specific place on the back of her shoulder: Crying:)* Do you see it? *(Pause.)* Daniel Edward Landon. *(He stares at her, at the tattoo, at his own name. A whisper, desperate, aching:)* Do you see it? *(And he wants to say something. He truly does. But, that is not his mission here. So, instead — the Young Soldier moves toward the wash basin. He lifts a final, full bucket of water — and pours it into the basin, as before. As he does so — Ben approaches. During the preceding, Ben has put on the white shirt, black tie, and glasses. Salyer now kneels on the ground where the Young Soldier left her — her back to us, her tattoos exposed. Her head buried in her hands. Ben stands directly behind the wash basin. The Young Soldier stands immediately next to him.)*

THE YOUNG SOLDIER. Your remarks, Mr. Secretary — have you prepared them?

BEN. No.

THE YOUNG SOLDIER. *(Firm.)* It's time, Mr. Secretary.

BEN. I cannot ... find words to express ... what lies in my heart today.

THE YOUNG SOLDIER. Go on.

BEN. No — don't you see — *(The Young Soldier places his hand firmly on Ben's shoulder — causing Ben to kneel directly behind the basin —)*

THE YOUNG SOLDIER. Go *on.*

BEN. *(With passion.)* All the evidence of history … suggests that man is, indeed, a rational animal … but with a near-infinite capacity for *folly* — *(And in one quick, powerful motion, the Young Soldier plunges Ben's head down into the water. It's an emphatic act; a visceral, enforced baptism. He holds Ben's head firmly underwater for a long moment — then yanks it up and out of the water —*

As his head emerges:) A man's history seems largely a halting, but persistent effort to raise his reason above his animal nature — *(Again, Ben's head is plunged down into the water for a long moment — and yanked back up again. A final plea, a cry:)* He draws blueprints for Utopia — but he never quite *gets it built* — *(Again, Ben's head is plunged down into the water — and held there for one long, final, aching moment [so long, in fact, that we may begin to fear the Young Soldier has come to drown him], but then: Ben's head is yanked back up again.*

Ben gasps for breath — wipes water from his face — and stares up at the Young Soldier who looms over him.

The Young Soldier looks at Ben, then: nods. And, after a final look at Salyer, the Young Soldier leaves the yard and is gone.

Silence. Ben slowly stands. He approaches her. She turns and meets his eye. A moment. Just the two of them.

Ben lowers the Young Soldier's dog tag into Salyer's hand. She takes it, staring up at him. Ben stands before her. And he simply says:) I'm sorry. *(There it is. Finally.*

Music plays: It might very well be that wailing Peter Green guitar solo from "Black Magic Woman" — the EARLY Fleetwood Mac version, of course.*

Ben is gone into the trailer — and Salyer into the night, as —

Lights shift from the moonlight of night to the orange glow of early morning. Music continues, as —

The door to the trailer opens and Lorraine emerges. She steps into the yard — retrieves her purse and flask of whiskey — and takes a good long look around, as —

Music fades out. The door opens again: It's Ben, just barely awake. He's got a coffee pot and mug in his hand.)

LORRAINE. Rise and shine. Morning has broken and it's foggy as hell.

---

* See Special Note on Songs and Recordings on copyright page.

BEN. Give it an hour. It'll burn off.

LORRAINE. I'm outta here. If you see the pin cushion, tell her I said goodbye. *(Re: the coffee.)* Pour me a cup of that, would you? *(Off his look.)* I like the smell. *(Ben pours coffee. Hands the mug to Lorraine. Then, Ben starts back into the trailer —)* Which one were you?

BEN. *(Stops.)* Huh?

LORRAINE. On that road — which soldier? *(He stares at her. Simply.)*

BEN. All of them. *(Ben turns and goes inside. Silence. Lorraine smells the steam from the coffee, and then … she sets the [untouched] cup of coffee in a prominent spot in the yard. And Salyer — entering from the shadows — sees Lorraine do this.)*

SALYER. Take me home. *(Lorraine looks up. Sees her.)*

LORRAINE. *(Simply.)* I'll be in the car. *(And Lorraine leaves, passing — Jeeter, who enters with purpose, carrying his backpack.)*

JEETER. Morning, Lorraine. *(But Lorraine doesn't even look up. Just walks past him. And is gone. To Lorraine's back:)* Oh, I'm peachy — thanks for asking.

SALYER. Jeeter, listen, I need to talk to you —

JEETER. *(Overlapping, get it said right now:)* Okay — enough *quests* — I promise — I'm done with all these stupid *quests* — wherever you want to go, it's good by me — I'll settle down, buy khaki pants, drive a Volvo — just say the word, Sal, and I'll do it —

SALYER. *(Touching his chest, stopping him.)* Keep going, Jeeter. On all your quests. *Keep going* —

JEETER. *But, Sal* —

SALYER. *(Overlapping.)* — and *don't look back.* That's what I want.

JEETER. *(Pause.)* And so I'm — what?! — just another name that gets *tattooed on your arm?*

SALYER. *(Simply.)* No. The thing is: You're not. *(She touches his face a final time. And as he reaches for her — to hold her, embrace her — She is gone. Jeeter stands there for a long moment. Then he winds up and hurls the backpack to the ground: BOOM, just as — Ben opens the door.)*

JEETER. *(Pause.)* Hey.

BEN. Hey.

JEETER. Thought maybe you'd left, too.

BEN. *(Re: his beat-up yard.)* And give up all *this*? *(Jeeter reaches into his pocket and pulls out some bills in a money clip. Hands this to Ben.)*

JEETER. Here's your money. Five hundred even. If you want interest compounded yearly, you're screwed. That's all you're getting.

BEN. *(Flat.)* Thanks.

JEETER. Now, we're even, right?

BEN. And this book of yours —

JEETER. Ben, listen —

BEN. When'll that be out?

JEETER. *(Beat.)* They say it'll be out by Christmas. *(Ben stares at him. Re: the suitcase:)* Don't forget the flag. He wanted you to have it. *(Now: Jeeter moves toward his JUST STOP sign. Lifts it.)*

BEN. Where now?

JEETER. Huh?

BEN. What is the *plan?*

JEETER. Portland. Seattle. Vancouver. Enough is enough.

BEN. They'll never stop, Jeeter. You know that.

JEETER. I know that. *(Beat.)* But I still gotta do it. *(Jeeter picks up his backpack. Looks back at Ben.)* Well: There it is. *(Beat.)* There it just no-doubt *is.* *(Silence. Jeeter waits for Ben to say something. And all he gets is this:)*

BEN. *(Simple.)* See you. *(It's over. Jeeter leaves, carrying the sign. Moving on. And —*

    Music plays, full and strong: It is no doubt something like Mr. Dylan's "Hard Rain's A-Gonna Fall." *

    Ben stands there for a long moment. Looks around his yard. Then he goes to the suitcase. Opens it. And removes the folded American flag.

    He holds the flag in front of him — staring at it. He looks up in the direction of his flagpole. Pause.

    He does not approach the flagpole. Instead: He walks to the ironing board.

    He sets the flag at one end of the board. And he slowly unfolds the flag along the length of the ironing board.

    Then: Ben opens the flag fully — so that it drapes the ironing board like a casket.

    Music continues, builds. Ben stares down at the flag. Smooths it with his fingers. And now ... it hits him. He bows his head, his eyes red and wet, gripping the ironing board with both hands. Holding on.

    Then: He raises his head. And: He reaches for his iron. Turns it on.

    And, as the music plays out, long and loud —

    Ben begins — slowly, carefully, expertly — to iron the flag.

    A man alone in his yard. And it's morning. And that's enough.

---

* See Special Note on Songs and Recordings on copyright page.

We'll leave it here. Just some days out of some people's lives. The things that can happen. A friendship ends; a war does not. In a thousand rooms it's the same. For now, though, this is all we've got.

See you.)

End of Play

PROPERTY LIST

Bottles of beer
White shirt, iron
Suitcase with small framed picture, necktie, suit coat, eyeglasses in case, American flag
Buckets of water
Piece of white paper
Large sign
Weathered backpack with snow globe
Tire iron
Official binder with five black-and-white photos
Bottle of whiskey, two glasses
Coffee pot, two mugs
6 doughnuts
Chips
Joint
Purse with flask
Glasses
Dog tags
Money, money clip

SOUND EFFECTS

Crickets
Helicopters
Jet
Mortar fire
Wind
Birds

SOUND

The author strongly suggests using the sound design by Rob Milburn and Michael Bodeen which was featured in the McCarter Theatre premiere and the subsequent Steppenwolf production of the play. For information, please contact:

Milburn/Bodeen Music and Sound Design
2730 W. Morse Ave.
Chicago, IL 60645
Tel. 773-338-1973
milbomusic1999@mac.com

NEW PLAYS

★ **GUARDIANS by Peter Morris.** In this unflinching look at war, a disgraced American soldier discloses the truth about Abu Ghraib prison, and a clever English journalist reveals how he faked a similar story for the London tabloids. "Compelling, sympathetic and powerful." *–NY Times.* "Sends you into a state of moral turbulence." *–Sunday Times (UK).* "Nothing short of remarkable." *–Village Voice.* [1M, 1W] ISBN: 978-0-8222-2177-7

★ **BLUE DOOR by Tanya Barfield.** Three generations of men (all played by one actor), from slavery through Black Power, challenge Lewis, a tenured professor of mathematics, to embark on a journey combining past and present. "A teasing flare for words." *–Village Voice.* "Unfailingly thought-provoking." *–LA Times.* "The play moves with the speed and logic of a dream." *–Seattle Weekly.* [2M] ISBN: 978-0-8222-2209-5

★ **THE INTELLIGENT DESIGN OF JENNY CHOW by Rolin Jones.** This irreverent "techno-comedy" chronicles one brilliant woman's quest to determine her heritage and face her fears with the help of her astounding creation called Jenny Chow. "Boldly imagined." *–NY Times.* "Fantastical and funny." *–Variety.* "Harvests many laughs and finally a few tears." *–LA Times.* [3M, 3W] ISBN: 978-0-8222-2071-8

★ **SOUVENIR by Stephen Temperley.** Florence Foster Jenkins, a wealthy society eccentric, suffers under the delusion that she is a great coloratura soprano—when in fact the opposite is true. "Hilarious and deeply touching. Incredibly moving and breathtaking." *–NY Daily News.* "A sweet love letter of a play." *–NY Times.* "Wildly funny. Completely charming." *–Star-Ledger.* [1M, 1W] ISBN: 978-0-8222-2157-9

★ **ICE GLEN by Joan Ackermann.** In this touching period comedy, a beautiful poetess dwells in idyllic obscurity on a Berkshire estate with a band of unlikely cohorts. "A beautifully written story of nature and change." *–Talkin' Broadway.* "A lovely play which will leave you with a lot to think about." *–CurtainUp.* "Funny, moving and witty." *–Metroland (Boston).* [4M, 3W] ISBN: 978-0-8222-2175-3

★ **THE LAST DAYS OF JUDAS ISCARIOT by Stephen Adly Guirgis.** Set in a time-bending, darkly comic world between heaven and hell, this play reexamines the plight and fate of the New Testament's most infamous sinner. "An unforced eloquence that finds the poetry in lowdown street talk." *–NY Times.* "A real jaw-dropper." *–Variety.* "An extraordinary play." *–Guardian (UK).* [10M, 5W] ISBN: 978-0-8222-2082-4

DRAMATISTS PLAY SERVICE, INC.
440 Park Avenue South, New York, NY 10016 212-683-8960 Fax 212-213-1539
postmaster@dramatists.com www.dramatists.com

NEW PLAYS

★ **THE GREAT AMERICAN TRAILER PARK MUSICAL music and lyrics by David Nehls, book by Betsy Kelso.** Pippi, a stripper on the run, has just moved into Armadillo Acres, wreaking havoc among the tenants of Florida's most exclusive trailer park. "Adultery, strippers, murderous ex-boyfriends, Costco and the Ice Capades. Undeniable fun." *–NY Post.* "Joyful and unashamedly vulgar." *–The New Yorker.* "Sparkles with treasure." *–New York Sun.* [2M, 5W] ISBN: 978-0-8222-2137-1

★ **MATCH by Stephen Belber.** When a young Seattle couple meet a prominent New York choreographer, they are led on a fraught journey that will change their lives forever. "Uproariously funny, deeply moving, enthralling theatre." *–NY Daily News.* "Prolific laughs and ear-to-ear smiles." *–NY Magazine.* [2M, 1W] ISBN: 978-0-8222-2020-6

★ **MR. MARMALADE by Noah Haidle.** Four-year-old Lucy's imaginary friend, Mr. Marmalade, doesn't have much time for her—not to mention he has a cocaine addiction and a penchant for pornography. "Alternately hilarious and heartbreaking." *–The New Yorker.* "A mature and accomplished play." *–LA Times.* "Scathingly observant comedy." *–Miami Herald.* [4M, 2W] ISBN: 978-0-8222-2142-5

★ **MOONLIGHT AND MAGNOLIAS by Ron Hutchinson.** Three men cloister themselves as they work tirelessly to reshape a screenplay that's just not working—*Gone with the Wind.* "Consumers of vintage Hollywood insider stories will eat up Hutchinson's diverting conjecture." *–Variety.* "A lot of fun." *–NY Post.* "A Hollywood dream-factory farce." *–Chicago Sun-Times.* [3M, 1W] ISBN: 978-0-8222-2084-8

★ **THE LEARNED LADIES OF PARK AVENUE by David Grimm, translated and freely adapted from Molière's *Les Femmes Savantes.*** Dicky wants to marry Betty, but her mother's plan is for Betty to wed a most pompous man. "A brave, brainy and barmy revision." *–Hartford Courant.* "A rare but welcome bird in contemporary theatre." *–New Haven Register.* "Roll over Cole Porter." *–Boston Globe.* [5M, 5W] ISBN: 978-0-8222-2135-7

★ **REGRETS ONLY by Paul Rudnick.** A sparkling comedy of Manhattan manners that explores the latest topics in marriage, friendships and squandered riches. "One of the funniest quip-meisters on the planet." *–NY Times.* "Precious moments of hilarity. Devastatingly accurate political and social satire." *–BackStage.* "Great fun." *–CurtainUp.* [3M, 3W] ISBN: 978-0-8222-2223-1

DRAMATISTS PLAY SERVICE, INC.
440 Park Avenue South, New York, NY 10016 212-683-8960 Fax 212-213-1539
postmaster@dramatists.com www.dramatists.com

NEW PLAYS

★ **AFTER ASHLEY by Gina Gionfriddo.** A teenager is unwillingly thrust into the national spotlight when a family tragedy becomes talk-show fodder. "A work that virtually any audience would find accessible." *–NY Times.* "Deft character-ization and caustic humor." *–NY Sun.* "A smart satirical drama." *–Variety.* [4M, 2W] ISBN: 978-0-8222-2099-2

★ **THE RUBY SUNRISE by Rinne Groff.** Twenty-five years after Ruby struggles to realize her dream of inventing the first television, her daughter faces similar battles of faith as she works to get Ruby's story told on network TV. "Measured and intelligent, optimistic yet clear-eyed." *–NY Magazine.* "Maintains an exciting sense of ingenuity." *–Village Voice.* "Sinuous theatrical flair." *–Broadway.com.* [3M, 4W] ISBN: 978-0-8222-2140-1

★ **MY NAME IS RACHEL CORRIE taken from the writings of Rachel Corrie, edited by Alan Rickman and Katharine Viner.** This solo piece tells the story of Rachel Corrie who was killed in Gaza by an Israeli bulldozer set to demol-ish a Palestinian home. "Heartbreaking urgency. An invigoratingly detailed por-trait of a passionate idealist." *–NY Times.* "Deeply authentically human." *–USA Today.* "A stunning dramatization." *–CurtainUp.* [1W] ISBN: 978-0-8222-2222-4

★ **ALMOST, MAINE by John Cariani.** This charming midwinter night's dream of a play turns romantic clichés on their ear as it chronicles the painfully hilarious amorous adventures (and misadventures) of residents of a remote northern town that doesn't quite exist. "A whimsical approach to the joys and perils of romance." *–NY Times.* "Sweet, poignant and witty." *–NY Daily News.* "Aims for the heart by way of the funny bone." *–Star-Ledger.* [2M, 2W] ISBN: 978-0-8222-2156-2

★ **Mitch Albom's TUESDAYS WITH MORRIE by Jeffrey Hatcher and Mitch Albom, based on the book by Mitch Albom.** The true story of Brandeis University professor Morrie Schwartz and his relationship with his stu-dent Mitch Albom. "A touching, life-affirming, deeply emotional drama." *–NY Daily News.* "You'll laugh. You'll cry." *–Variety.* "Moving and powerful." *–NY Post.* [2M] ISBN: 978-0-8222-2188-3

★ **DOG SEES GOD: CONFESSIONS OF A TEENAGE BLOCKHEAD by Bert V. Royal.** An abused pianist and a pyromaniac ex-girlfriend contribute to the teen-angst of America's most hapless kid. "A welcome antidote to the notion that the *Peanuts* gang provides merely American cuteness." *–NY Times.* "Hysterically funny." *–NY Post.* "The *Peanuts* kids have finally come out of their shells." *–Time Out.* [4M, 4W] ISBN: 978-0-8222-2152-4

DRAMATISTS PLAY SERVICE, INC.
440 Park Avenue South, New York, NY 10016 212-683-8960 Fax 212-213-1539
postmaster@dramatists.com www.dramatists.com

NEW PLAYS

★ **RABBIT HOLE by David Lindsay-Abaire.** Winner of the 2007 Pulitzer Prize. Becca and Howie Corbett have everything a couple could want until a life-shattering accident turns their world upside down. "An intensely emotional examination of grief, laced with wit." *–Variety.* "A transcendent and deeply affecting new play." *–Entertainment Weekly.* "Painstakingly beautiful." *–BackStage.* [2M, 3W] ISBN: 978-0-8222-2154-8

★ **DOUBT, A Parable by John Patrick Shanley.** Winner of the 2005 Pulitzer Prize and Tony Award. Sister Aloysius, a Bronx school principal, takes matters into her own hands when she suspects the young Father Flynn of improper relations with one of the male students. "All the elements come invigoratingly together like clockwork." *–Variety.* "Passionate, exquisite, important, engrossing." *–NY Newsday.* [1M, 3W] ISBN: 978-0-8222-2219-4

★ **THE PILLOWMAN by Martin McDonagh.** In an unnamed totalitarian state, an author of horrific children's stories discovers that someone has been making his stories come true. "A blindingly bright black comedy." *–NY Times.* "McDonagh's least forgiving, bravest play." *–Variety.* "Thoroughly startling and genuinely intimidating." *–Chicago Tribune.* [4M, 5 bit parts (2M, 1W, 1 boy, 1 girl)] ISBN: 978-0-8222-2100-5

★ **GREY GARDENS book by Doug Wright, music by Scott Frankel, lyrics by Michael Korie.** The hilarious and heartbreaking story of Big Edie and Little Edie Bouvier Beale, the eccentric aunt and cousin of Jacqueline Kennedy Onassis, once bright names on the social register who became East Hampton's most notorious recluses. "An experience no passionate theatergoer should miss." *–NY Times.* "A unique and unmissable musical." *–Rolling Stone.* [4M, 3W, 2 girls] ISBN: 978-0-8222-2181-4

★ **THE LITTLE DOG LAUGHED by Douglas Carter Beane.** Mitchell Green could make it big as the hot new leading man in Hollywood if Diane, his agent, could just keep him in the closet. "Devastatingly funny." *–NY Times.* "An out-and-out delight." *–NY Daily News.* "Full of wit and wisdom." *–NY Post.* [2M, 2W] ISBN: 978-0-8222-2226-2

★ **SHINING CITY by Conor McPherson.** A guilt-ridden man reaches out to a therapist after seeing the ghost of his recently deceased wife. "Haunting, inspired and glorious." *–NY Times.* "Simply breathtaking and astonishing." *–Time Out.* "A thoughtful, artful, absorbing new drama." *–Star-Ledger.* [3M, 1W] ISBN: 978-0-8222-2187-6

DRAMATISTS PLAY SERVICE, INC.
440 Park Avenue South, New York, NY 10016 212-683-8960 Fax 212-213-1539
postmaster@dramatists.com www.dramatists.com